the Divine ADVENTURE

ST. TERESA OF AVILA'S JOURNEYS AND FOUNDATIONS

St. Teresa "la Andariega" at the Monastery of the Incarnation, Ávila

Sculpture by Fernando Cruz Solis (1923–1991)

Photo © Lawrence Lew, O.P.

the Divine ADVENTURE

ST. TERESA OF AVILA'S JOURNEYS AND FOUNDATIONS

Tomás Álvarez, O.C.D., and Fernando Domingo, O.C.D.

With an Introduction by Kieran Kavanaugh, O.C.D.

Translated by Christopher O'Mahony

With additional translation and adaptation
by Patricia Lynn Morrison

ICS Publications
Institute of Carmelite Studies
Washington, D.C.

ICS Publications
2131 Lincoln Road, N.E.
Washington, DC 20002-1199
www.icspublications.org.

Cover photo: St. Teresa "la Andariega" at the Monastery of the Incarnation, Ávila, Spain; bronze sculpture by Fernando Cruz Solis (1923–1991).

Photo © Lawrence Lew, O.P.; published with permission

Book and cover design and pagination by Rose Design & Illustration

Produced and printed in the United States of America

Library of Congress Control Number: 2015938850

ISBN 978-1-939272-26-3

Contents

Translators' Note and Abbreviations

The numerous quotations from St. Teresa's works in this book have been translated afresh from the original Spanish. The abbreviated reference after each quotation is to be understood as follows: the letter stands for one of her works, the first number for a chapter, and the second number for a paragraph.

The *Letters* are listed by letter number, followed by paragraph number. (Letters, published in two volumes, are identified consecutively.)

The works cited are abbreviated thus:

   F *The Book of the Foundations*
   L *The Book of Her Life*
 Ltr *Letters*
   P *Poetry*
 ST *Spiritual Testimonies*
WP *The Way of Perfection*

Additional source materials from St. Teresa's companions and contemporary biographers are cited after direct quotations when we have been able to identify them. Most of these works are available only in Spanish. Because of the variety of editions and publishers of these materials, we have listed only the work and chapter (when available), but not page numbers.

In the text we have abbreviated them by a single word descriptor:

Autobiografía	Autobiography of Anne of St. Bartholomew
Recreaciónes	[*Libro de* . . .] Book of Recreations by María de San José
Relación/es	The Relations by Anne of St. Bartholomew
Peregrinación	The Pilgrimage of Anastasius by Jerome Gracián
Vida	The Life of St. Teresa of Jesus by Julian of Ávila

From the Editor

This book, published in Spanish in 2012 as *Por Los Caminos de Teresa*, is a revised and expanded version of a similar work co-published in multiple languages in 1982 to commemorate the fourth centenary of St. Teresa's death. That English edition was titled *Saint Teresa of Avila: A Spiritual Adventure* and was a joint publication of Monte Carmelo, the Discalced Carmelite publishing house in Burgos, Spain, and ICS Publications, the publishing house of the Discalced Carmelites of the Washington Province in the United States.

Like the earlier English edition of *A Spiritual Adventure*, this new edition in its present title also incorporates much of the earlier translation done by Christopher O'Mahony. Where the 2015 edition includes new or updated material not available previously, this has been added in a new translation and American English idiom.

Por Los Caminos de Teresa was originally intended for a Spanish-speaking readership that would be familiar with many of the details of Spanish and European history and geography, as well as Carmelite history and usage. Many English-speaking readers, however, might not have this familiarity or historical background. In this English edition, then, we have expanded on some notes or added further explanatory material to provide what we hope is helpful background and context for the reader. Similarly, to create a smoother text for English readers, we have sometimes omitted minor references that would be understood only by native Spaniards, or that are not provided in context.

Additionally, in the narrative, we have converted the measurements of leagues and kilometers to miles, and meters to feet. Due to restrictions of time and expense, we could not completely reconstruct the detailed graphics that chart St. Teresa's travels. Instead, we've aimed for a middle road: altitude, listed next to cities, has been converted to feet and placed in approximate location on the charts; the numbered vertical and horizontal headings (representing altitude and distance respectively) have been represented in feet and miles, respectively. It is our hope that the charts themselves, together with the mileage and altitude listings, will enable the English-speaking reader to better visualize the distances involved in St. Teresa's various journeys as well as the distances between one and another, and literally the "ups and downs" of the foundress's travels, ranging from mountainous heights to areas below sea level.

Wherever direct quotations from St. Teresa's works appear in the text, we have aimed to include appropriate citations for them. In some instances where the Spanish original or research does not permit us to provide a clear source for quotations from other personalities (Julian of Ávila, Anne of St. Bartholomew, Jerome Gracián, etc.) we have simply listed the name of the writer/narrator when this has been provided. Since the works of these persons are often not available in English (or in identifiable English editions), simply indicating the author seemed to be more helpful to the reader than adding notes or citations to works accessible only in Spanish or other non-English editions. When the title of these works is known in Spanish, we have included it with a one-word description; the full titles of these works and their authors are listed on the abbreviations page.

Finally, a word of appreciation. A book like this comes together only through the collaboration and contributions of many people working behind the scenes.

In the first place, ICS Publications thanks Monte Carmelo, our Discalced Carmelite publishing house in Burgos, Spain, for permission to make this valuable book available to English-speaking readers around the world during this fifth centenary year of St. Teresa's birth. Father Kieran Kavanaugh, O.C.D., publisher emeritus of ICS Publications and perhaps the foremost expert on St. Teresa in the English-speaking world, graciously and generously made time among his many ongoing projects to write the introduction to this English edition and also to research and reply to my many questions; my heartfelt thanks, Father Kieran!

Several editors, proofreaders, and colleagues who prefer to remain unnamed helped clarify inconsistencies, improve translations and wording, and researched facts and obscure terms with unfailing patience, humor, and grace. (Any errant errors that have managed to escape the corral, unfortunately, are mine.)

Last but certainly not least, we thank those whose creative and artistic skills remind us that, as Emerson wrote, "beauty is God's handwriting." These include three people in a special way: the internationally acclaimed photographer, Father Lawrence Lew, O.P., in Edinburgh, Scotland, for the use on the book's cover and frontispiece of his lovely photograph of St. Teresa's statue "la Andariega," outside the Monastery of the Incarnation in Ávila; and Carol and Eric Sawyer of Rose Design & Illustration, who regularly, with wonderful skill and talent (and patience through multiple revisions), work their magic on the covers, layout, and design of so many of our ICS Publications titles. We are greatly blessed, and we thank you all.

PATRICIA LYNN MORRISON
Editorial Director
ICS Publications

Introduction to the English-language Edition

In the nave of St. Peter's Basilica in Rome, among the statues of saints who were founders of religious orders, you will find one of St. Teresa of Ávila. Inscribed on its base are these words in Latin: *S. Teresia spiritualis Mater et Fundatrix*, "St. Teresa: spiritual mother and foundress."

Founding new monasteries was one of Teresa's charisms. The first foundation was St. Joseph in Ávila, recounted in *The Book of Her Life* (chaps. 32–36). When Father Giovanni Battista Rossi, the general of the Carmelite Order, visited Teresa's new monastery, she was worried about what he would say, since she had placed it under the jurisdiction of the bishop of Ávila. Instead, the Carmelite general was so pleased with what she had done that he gave her orders to found as many monasteries as "she had hairs on her head" (*Letters* 269.10), thus giving her under obedience the task of establishing additional monasteries. With these orders in mind, Teresa made her first departure from Ávila for a new foundation in Medina del Campo in 1567. This launched her further travels through many parts of Spain, where she established new monasteries in Malagón, Valladolid, Duruelo, Toledo, Pastrana, Salamanca, Alba de Tormes, Segovia, Beas, and Seville.

Soon complaints began to arise against these "scandalous" travels of Teresa. After all, she was a woman, and a cloistered one at that! Teresa herself, influenced by these criticisms, began to doubt: might she be better off if she were not out traveling the roads of Spain? These qualms were eased by words the Lord spoke to her: "While one is alive, progress doesn't come from trying to enjoy Me more but by trying to do My will" (*Spiritual Testimonies* 15). And as for what St. Paul said about women keeping silence in the churches, the Lord advised her, "Tell them they shouldn't follow just one part of Scripture but that they should look at other parts, and ask them if they can by chance tie My hands" (*Spiritual Testimonies* 15).

But the Lord's reassurances to Teresa notwithstanding, the complaints and grumbling about this "gadabout nun" continued. Even the papal nuncio, Nicolás Ormaneto, who had high esteem for Teresa, wrote a confidential note to Teresa's friend and supporter Jerome Gracián: "As for me I was never pleased with the manner, according to what I understand, in which the Madre Teresa goes about founding and visiting monasteries. For women who profess the regular life should stay within their houses and not be going here and there, since these visitations are a task that belongs to her male superiors, who can travel without giving scandal or be in danger. . . . Advise me about what you think and for the time being don't say anything about this to anyone, for I wouldn't want to sadden this good and holy Mother" (Tomás Alvarez, O.C.D., *Diccionario de Santa Teresa* [Burgos, Spain: Monte Carmelo, 2002], 1070–71).

These doubts about Teresa's activities increased even in the soul of the father general and of the general chapter of the Carmelite Order convened in Piacenza, Italy, in 1575. With these misgivings, fueled by all the criticism Teresa's travels had generated, the chapter officially ordered Teresa to stop making foundations and visiting them. In a word, she was ordered to give up traveling around Spain and to enclose herself in one of her monasteries. She replied frankly to the father general: "In these parts they have never understood, nor do they understand, the Council [of Trent] or *Moto proprio* as having taken away from prelates the authority to allow nuns to go outside to do things for the good of the order" (*Letters* 102.15). Still, she obeyed and returned from Andalusia to Castile, first going to Toledo and then to Ávila. Here she was met with the categorical disapproval of the new papal nuncio, Felipe Sega, who stigmatized her as a "restless vagabond" (*Letters* 269.3).

For these reasons, Teresa's traveling as foundress was suspended for four years (*Foundations* 28.1). Once the whirlwind of adversity had passed, Teresa again took up her travels and tasks as foundress, and she continued doing so until her last foundation in Burgos in 1582, a few months before she died.

Teresa had finished *The Book of Her Life*, in which she told the story of her first foundation, St. Joseph's in Ávila, and now continued in her inimitable way recounting in *The Book of the Foundations* the story of all her other foundations. In this present book we have a summary of all that Teresa endured in order to obey her father general's command to found as many monasteries she could. Though physically worn out, even up to the time of her death Teresa still held onto her dream of making another foundation, this one in Madrid. After everything was settled with her foundation in Burgos, on her way back to Ávila, where she was still prioress, she received orders by her acting superior to go to Alba de Tormes because the Duchess of Alba wanted to see her again. Exhausted, Teresa arrived in Alba on September 20. Nine days later she went to bed so seriously ill that she was never to get up again; she died five days later at the age of sixty-seven.

In this book, in addition to the enjoyable account of Teresa's work as foundress, we have a further treat. When we read in Teresa's *Book of the Foundations* about her many trials in fulfilling the mission given to her by her father general, much is left to our imaginations about the events, places, and things of which she speaks. But this no longer has to be true. We have in this updated and expanded book, published for the fifth centenary of Teresa's birth, many photographs and illustrations of the monasteries she founded, a number of which are still in the same place and even in the same building as they were in her lifetime.

Unlike the friars, the Carmelite nuns founded by Teresa are notorious for saving things, and they did so very carefully with everything they possessed having reference to their mother foundress. As a result, we still have the original manuscripts of all Teresa's writings, as well as paintings she had commissioned for her hermitages in the garden and statues she brought with her for new foundations. Here, too, we see the walking stick she used and even the castanets and tambourine she played to enliven recreations with her nuns. We see the Communion windows through which the cloistered nuns received Communion and the parlors where Teresa spent time consulting about her spiritual life with Fray John of the Cross or about business matters with Fray Jerome Gracián. We see some of Spain's majestic castles that

Teresa would have glimpsed in her travels and which inspired some of her ideas for her masterpiece, *The Interior Castle*. In hundreds of color photos, many other objects and sites from Teresa's day make of this new fifth centenary edition not only an enjoyable read but also a remarkable, visual delight.

For those fortunate to visit the sites in Spain made famous by this exceptional saint and foundress, this book will be a wonderful souvenir and even a travel guide. But others also—devotees of St. Teresa, students of her works, and anyone with an interest in the life she established in her Discalced Carmelite monasteries and the spirituality she lived and taught—will find in *The Divine Adventure* an inspiring "armchair pilgrimage" into St. Teresa's world, wherever the reader lives.

Kieran Kavanaugh, O.C.D.
Discalced Carmelite Monastery
Washington, D.C.

March 28, 2015
500th anniversary of the birth
of St. Teresa of Jesus

Prologue to an Adventure

The aim of this book is to describe the glorious adventure on which St. Teresa of Jesus embarked when she answered the call to begin a reform of the Carmelites. Through it the reader can join her on the roads of Castile, La Mancha, and Andalusia and share the pain and the glory of this new birth.

It was a noble venture, conducted in a manner reminiscent of those saints whom Cervantes's Don Quixote met on his last expedition, people who caused him to exclaim, "These saints professed what I professed—they do battle. But the difference between them and me was that they were saints and fought in godly fashion, whereas I am a sinner and fight in human fashion." In godly fashion, but no less humanly for all that, Teresa traveled the roads of Spain, on muleback or by wagon, establishing Carmelite monasteries and their chapels. She spent the last fifteen years of her life doing that, and she had founded her first monastery in Ávila five years earlier still. So her founding activity spans twenty years in all, traveling in sunshine and in snow, in rain and cold alike. She was forty-seven when she started and sixty-seven when death cut short her last journey at Alba de Tormes, just when her cherished dream of founding in Madrid seemed about to be fulfilled.

Before we embark on this journey, it will be helpful for the reader to know something of the background to this adventure: those gray years in which Teresa laboriously laid the groundwork for her venture, and the horizons and landscape that formed her vision.

Teresa was born in Ávila on March 28, 1515, to Don Alonso de Cepeda and Doña Beatriz de Ahumada. When she began her founding activity she dropped these two surnames; henceforth she would choose to be known simply as Teresa *de Jesús*—Teresa of Jesus.

The family might be described as belonging to the gentry rather than the nobility, what the Spaniards called *hidalgos*. Don Alonso had twelve

Autograph of St. Teresa. She begins the account of the foundation of St. Joseph's (*Life* 32): "Chapter XXXII: tells how the Lord was pleased to carry her in spirit to a place in hell which she had merited for her sins. Describes a part of what was shown to her there. Begins to tell of the way and means whereby the monastery of St. Joseph, where she is now, was founded."

children, three girls and nine boys. In an era enthusiastic with conquest, riches, and adventure in the newly discovered Americas, not surprisingly all the sons sought fame and fortune across the seas. Their mother had died when Teresa was only thirteen and her sister Juana a newborn, so eventually there came a time when Don Alonso, Teresa, and little Juana were the only ones left at home.

From the balcony of the now nearly empty home, Teresa's inner vision scanned well beyond the skyline: to the Argentine where her favorite brother, Rodrigo—once so eager to accompany her to death and glory at the hands of the Moors—later died; to Ecuador and Peru where other brothers-become-conquistadors would fight and die; and to Mexico where friends of hers served the native peoples and returned home to tell of the great pastoral needs there. Her own physical horizons were so limited by comparison. There was her aborted effort to escape to martyrdom at the age of six or seven. The family had estates in nearby Gotarrendura, and a married sister lived some miles on the opposite side of Ávila. This was the farthest from

Coat of arms of the City of Ávila.
Beautiful bas relief in stone

home Teresa had ever traveled. Apart from where her flights of fancy took her, her world was a small one.

At twenty, Teresa too left home. As she recounts in her *Life*, "I remember that when I left my father's house it was with such heartbreak that death itself would not be worse; I left absolutely torn asunder."

She was leaving home forever, going to the Carmelite monastery of the Incarnation just outside the walls of Ávila. Another world, another home. Another family too, but a much larger one: some 150 in all, between nuns and boarders, young girls who hoped to become novices in maybe five or ten years' time. The community was very poor, in spite of the fact that all the noblest names in Ávila were to be found there.

Life at the Incarnation took its inspiration from Mount Carmel in the Holy Land, with its stories and legends reaching back to the Old Testament. As a religious institution, the Carmelites dated from the early 13th century. The monastery of the Incarnation, however, was no more than about fifty years old when it opened its doors to Teresa.

Two years of monastic apprenticeship followed. Then, at twenty-two, Teresa made her final vows. Shortly afterward, she was struck down with a mysterious illness that slowly wasted her body and very nearly ended her life entirely. In the summer of 1539 she had a complete physical breakdown.

"I had a seizure which left me unconscious for almost four days," she tells us, and, when she regained her senses, "I was in such a state that only the Lord knows what I went through: I had chewed my tongue to bits, my throat was choking me, I couldn't even swallow water. I seemed to be torn limb from limb, and was quite delirious. I was all curled up and unable to move . . . any more than if I was dead. . . . As far as I remember, I could move just one finger of my right hand" (L 6.1).

This illness was the starting point of a very important aspect of Teresa's life. You could call it her physical history, perhaps. She retained her natural beauty and charm, but from now on she would always be very physically fragile. One of her triumphs was to constantly rise above the state of her health and conduct her affairs from the command post of her indomitable spirit.

To regain her health, Teresa had to leave her monastery for a while. She also left it for the occasional short and exceptional visit. But mostly she just lived at the Incarnation; her traveling was inward.

The world Teresa set out to discover and conquer was the inner world of her own soul. She called her journey "the way of prayer," or as the title of one of her books has it, "the way of perfection." The writings of the "spirituals" of the Franciscan reform movement were her starting point, and she followed the road diligently right up to the heights of the "experience of God."

It was an uphill struggle, with periods of backsliding, weariness, and temptations to abandon the quest and return to the broad, comfortable surroundings she had left. She even gave into these and, ashamed of herself, quit the undertaking for a while; she wasn't yet ready for that unconditional fidelity to the inner call that beckoned her on to the fullness of life.

Teresa devoted a whole book—her *Life*—to the story of these ups and downs: twenty years trying to learn to walk!

Then her father died. This seems to have acted as a spur to face God again. Ten years of further uphill struggle followed. And then, at thirty-nine, she was suddenly there, so to speak.

Two events mark her arrival at the top: a very personal encounter between Teresa and Jesus, and the reading of St. Augustine's *Confessions*. Teresa regarded this date as that of her "conversion" and associated it with those two events.

She had reached the wonderful promised land of "experience of God"; it was 1554. As if she had been born again, with wings and new life, Teresa felt inwardly driven by *love* and the need to *do*. By the new light in her life she discovered the "interior castle." She rediscovered the meaning of life, the beauty of things, the dignity of the individual, the sublimity of friendship, and the true scale of values in all God's creation.

The phrase "what I see is like a dream" recurs several times in her writings. It was as if she had never seen or enjoyed things before. Her hour had come. Planning and finalizing her first foundation, St. Joseph's in Ávila, took from 1560 to 1562. In that same period she undertook her first long trip: she went to Toledo and stayed in that imperial city for six months. That brought her into contact with the high society of her time and marked the beginning of her world tour—a social world tour, that is, in which she gradually came to rub shoulders with all kinds of people from all levels of society and all walks of life. Among them were bankers, muleteers, merchants, boatmen, beggars, bishops, sacristans, *beatas*, theologians, country curates, dukes and duchesses, princes and princesses, and even a king and queen. To list names at this stage would be tedious; we will meet these people as their turn comes to share the stage with our heroine.

We are fortunate that at this distance in time we can look in on the world in which Teresa moved; in her letters no fewer than 1,000 people who crossed her path still pass before us.

Her social journey went hand in hand with her geographical travels, of course. When in 1567 she left St. Joseph's for her seemingly endless journeys on muleback or in her covered wagon, she had been a cloistered nun for thirty-two years. Outside, the Castilian landscape was still the same: holm oaks, poplars, wheat fields, fallow land, bleak moors. But the human landscape had changed radically. The sun had set on the Spanish empire and on the triumphal spirit of the generation of Charles V.

The new generation was nervous and tense; times were lean and problems many. The Spanish court had moved from Valladolid to Madrid. The Council of Trent had come and gone. The wars of religion had broken out again in France, and in Spain the forces of the Inquisition were definitely not a sign of well-being. The unity of Christendom and of Europe was broken and would stay broken. In Africa, the king of Portugal's odd attempt to revive the Crusades failed with his death. All of this pained Teresa in a very real way.

It was only now, in fact, that she really discovered Europe: France, the Netherlands, England, Germany, and "the Lutherans" became part of the ideal and focus of prayer in her Carmels. It was now that she became aware of the "great evils which beset the church" and began to feel them as if they hurt her physically: "To worry about anything else seems ridiculous," she remarked.

Teresa rediscovered the Americas too at this time, as she listened to the reports of the Franciscan missionary Alonso Maldonado of the millions of "Indians" whose souls were being lost in the newly colonized Mexico.

Her journeys were confined to her own country; the slow-moving wagons never covered more than twenty-five to thirty-five miles a day. These travels cannot be even remotely compared to those of St. Paul or St. Francis Xavier. Teresa never even reached the shores of the Mediterranean or of the Atlantic. The nearest she got to the sea was the view of the imperial fleet hoisting sail in Seville.

But as we've said, her spirit roamed freely in other landscapes and was open to the whole world. As she thought of the Americas, she wrote, "Those Indians have cost me no little suffering." She felt keen pain over Spain's war with Portugal. She placed her hope in the universal mission of the church on whose chessboard she was conscious that she was a minor yet indispensable piece.

Teresa was not destined to leave her native Spain in person, or even reach distant parts of it, such as the Basque country or Valencia. But she would reach the lands of her dreams and of her prayers through her daughters, and her words would reach them too.

If this book were to trace the path of her writings throughout the world, it would become a sizeable atlas, especially if we took into account all the languages into which they have been translated. In a way, Teresa is still traveling the world, dispensing her spirit in the bread of her word.

ÁVILA Dates and Events concerning the First Foundation

1560

Two mystical graces: the vision of Christ and another of hell, recounted by Teresa in the *Life* 27 and 32.

1560
Spring–Summer

Gathering of friends in Mother Teresa's cell in the Incarnation. Genesis of the idea of founding a poor convent.

August 4

Don Álvaro de Mendoza is named bishop of Ávila.

1561
August 15

In a vision, the Blessed Virgin reassures Teresa about the future of her reform and the monasteries she will found (L 33.14–15).

December

Teresa's brother Lorenzo sends her money from Quito, Ecuador. The saint writes him a letter (12/23/1561). The provincial orders her to travel to Toledo (12/24/1561).

1562

Teresa spends six months in Toledo, in the palace of Doña Luisa de la Cerda.

Teresa obtains a brief from the Holy See's Sacred Penitentiary in Rome authorizing her to found monasteries.

June

In Toledo, Teresa completes the first version of her *Life*.

August 24

Founding of the Carmel of St. Joseph in Ávila. Summoned by the prioress of the Incarnation, Teresa leaves the new convent.

August 25

The Ávila city council files suit against the foundation. August 29: "All the estates of the city" are required to oppose Mother Teresa and her convent.

October 19

Death of St. Peter of Alcántara.

December 5

From Rome, Teresa is granted the brief permitting her to found monasteries in poverty (without income).

December 6

Death of the Carmelite general, Nicolás Audet. Juan Bautista Rubeo (Rossi) succeeds him as vicar (12/19); Rubeo will be elected general on May 21, 1564.

1563
July 23

Teresa's friend María de Jesús founds La Imagen Carmel in Alcalá.

August 22

The provincial grants Teresa permission to reside at St. Joseph's.

1565
July 17

The bull of Pope Pius IV is issued in favor of St. Joseph's.

Last months

Teresa completes the final version of her *Life*.

Important Contemporary Events

1558

Emperor Charles V dies at Yuste (Extremadura), Spain.

1559

The Inquisition publishes the *Index of Forbidden Books* (by Valdés), including many of those used by Mother Teresa.

1562

Massacre at Vassy, France. Religious wars break out again in France.

1562–1563

Last session of the Council of Trent.

1563

Construction begins on the royal palace of El Escorial near Madrid.

Exterior of the Monastery of San José (St. Joseph); drawing by Hye Hoys (1866–1867)

Ávila

ST. JOSEPH'S MONASTERY

AUGUST 24, 1562

Here is the first monastery founded by St. Teresa. It looks like a scale model of its more grandiose contemporaries. One might say it was planned according to the scale of the Gospel; and, indeed, the Master's various comparisons to the Kingdom fit it admirably: the mustard seed, the leaven, the light on the lamp stand, the salt of the earth.

The river of history has many sources, all of them well-known, but they are all fed from chapter 32 of St. Teresa's own autobiography, the *Life*. It begins, "After the Lord had been granting me the favors I have been speaking of, and many others, for quite some time, I was praying one day when suddenly, I know not how, I seemed to be plunged into hell" (L 32.1).

We appreciate the beauty of light only by contrast with darkness, or the gift of health only when faced with tragic illness. So too Teresa, faced with this terrifying vision, decided to leave behind all deviation from the straight path, to flee the compromises of life, and devote herself wholeheartedly to being grateful for her own salvation and to bringing others to it.

She hardly noticed hardships any more. "I find everything easy," she said, "compared to one moment of what I suffered there . . . I would gladly give a thousand lives to spare even one person such terrible torments" (L 32.1).

Some means had to be found, and quickly, to avoid such evil and procure so great a good. She found it. Teresa would begin by reforming herself, by being fully consistent with her Carmelite vocation, by observing the Rule with all the perfection of which she was capable.

Teresa realized that living in the Monastery of the Incarnation with some 180 nuns was like belonging to a respectable club. They were good women, of course, even servants of God, but nothing more. Good intentions are not enough for self-reform. Social pressures made themselves felt in the monastery and came from the city outside. The nuns found a thousand and one perfectly lawful reasons for going and coming with the same frequency as the multitude of visitors who were always around the place. They had permission too to observe a mitigated version of the Rule. The monastery, to quote Teresa herself, was "a pretty comfortable place, being large and spacious" (L 32.1).

Besides, Teresa was not the only one to feel the way she did about things. She had often discussed the state of the monastery with her close friends. And finally, one September evening in 1560, those friends and relations—some of them nuns and some laywomen—were together again in Teresa's cell. No doubt they talked of many things, but inevitably their favorite topic came up again: the need for more solitude, and their desire for a new style of monastic life. A community of well over a hundred nuns, they felt, was not conducive to that intimate friendship that included everyone, free from cliques, and from the impersonal atmosphere created by a governing structure designed for large numbers. They were also convinced that so much contact with outsiders was not exactly a help. A young nun, María de Ocampo, a niece of St. Teresa's, spoke for all of them: "All right then, let's all go and start another kind of life, something more solitary like the hermits had."

The suggestion could not have fallen on better ground. It was exactly what Teresa had been thinking about—just what she wanted.

It was one of Teresa's most cherished convictions that if quality was preferable to quantity in most things, it was paramount where religious persons were concerned. She was a firm believer in the effectiveness of the select group. Few but committed. As she so incisively put it, "One person of quality will do more than many who are lacking in it" (WP 3.5). She believed too in the advantages of the small group; all know one another and communicate directly, and they are so few that it would be "brutal" not to love one another. The moment had come to tackle the task, to give wings to their restlessness and body to their ideas.

It was shortly after this that Teresa had a visit from Doña Guiomar de Ulloa, a close friend with whom she shared her troubles and her hopes. Half

Convent of Our Lady of Grace where Teresa lived as a boarder at the age of 15–16

The historic Church of St. Teresa, known as "La Santa," at the Discalced friars' monastery in Ávila

The Monastery of the Incarnation

jokingly (and wholly in earnest), Teresa told her of her dreams of a little monastery. Far from taking it as a joke, Doña Guiomar became quite taken with the idea and promptly promised to provide the money for the venture.

Things moved quickly after that. Teresa consulted learned men and friends, and found everybody in agreement. The Carmelite provincial, Father Angel de Salazar, was delighted to receive the proposed house under his obedience. Teresa's Jesuit confessor, Father Baltasar Álvarez, could see God's hand on the project. Father Pedro Ibáñez, a Dominican friar universally esteemed for learning and holiness, gave it his unreserved support. And that great ascetic, St. Peter of Alcántara, was more enthusiastic than anyone.

But the works of God—and this had all the signs of one—are never accomplished by a unanimous vote. No sooner had word of the project gotten around the city than all hell broke loose on the principal people involved.

The Council of Ávila, a city as proud of its noble lineage as it was short of money, refused even to consider the very idea of a monastery that would be supported by alms. The nuns of the Monastery of the Incarnation, Teresa's sisters, were offended: she could serve God just as well here; there were lots of nuns who were holier than she, and they needed money too. On and on ran the complaints. The preachers thundered, and the ordinary people whispered against this nun who, under pretext of greater perfection, was surely up to no good.

It never rains but it pours. Now Doña Guiomar discovered she didn't have enough money to build the monastery, nor could she freely dispose of what she did have.

The Carmelite provincial, fearful of worse to come, caved in before the onslaught. Not only did he withdraw his support for Teresa, but also he sent her off to Toledo to comfort a noble widow. Her confessor told her to forget the whole thing.

There's a saying that a stool needs only three legs. Fortunately, the controversial foundress had three sterling supports: her own resolute determination; the loyalty of her closest friends; and, above and before all, her God. His was undeniably the leading role in this whole drama. The Lord left Teresa in no doubt about his will; powerfully, insistently, he said, Yes, go ahead. As Teresa testifies, "His Majesty insisted I strive for it with all my strength, and promised me it would be done. . . . [He said] I was not to think that He was not being served in monasteries that were moderate in observance; that the world would be a sad place were it not for religious" (L 32.11).

When opposition intensified, the Lord was in control: "He told me not to weary myself . . . to do what my confessor told me by being silent for the time being" (L 33.3).

When she thought the house she bought was too small for a monastery, the Lord chided her: "I've told you to go on as best you can. Oh, the greed of the human race to think you will lack land! How often have I slept beneath the skies for want of a place to go!" (L 33.12).

Kitchen in St. Teresa's suite of rooms at the Incarnation

When she wasn't sure whether or not she should give in on the question of income, Jesus set her straight: "On no account was she to neglect to found it in poverty" (L 35.6).

Later, when she had finally managed to get the monastery established and people came shouting at the nuns in an effort to make them leave the place, the Lord said, "Don't you know I'm powerful; what are you afraid of?" He assured her that the work "would not be undone" (L 36.16).

But lest the reader tire of quotations about the Lord's constant intervention, let's sum them all up in this last one: he assures Teresa "that this house was a paradise for His pleasure" (L 35.12).

We are still in 1561, and the first move has yet to be made. But with such comprehensive insurance, there was no holding Teresa back. Besides, she could still count on those loyal friends, and she proceeded to organize them in a way that did her prowess at chess proud. To name only the more outstanding among them, they were Fathers Pedro Ibáñez; Baltasar Álvarez; Peter of Alcántara, whom we've already mentioned; Master Gaspar Daza;

The church of the Carmelite monastery of St. Joseph in Ávila, "Las Madres"

a holy layman, Francisco de Salcedo; and her future standard-bearer and chaplain, Julian of Ávila.

Since secrecy was of the essence, Teresa asked her brother-in-law Juan de Ovalle, who lived in Alba, to buy a house in Ávila as if it were for himself and to live in it while remodeling was being carried out. That was in the summer of 1561.

After that, things began to come together quite rapidly. Enough money for the project arrived from her brother Lorenzo in South America. Teresa returned from Toledo where she had made some very good friends. The danger of being elected prioress of the Incarnation appeared to have passed. And finally, Gaspar Daza and Peter of Alcántara obtained the required permission from Rome and from Bishop Álvaro de Mendoza of Ávila for a monastery founded on alms. The latter also agreed that it should be directly subject to himself.

And so we come to the joyous and unforgettable day of August 24, 1562. Dawn had scarcely broken over the highest ramparts of the city walls when a shrill little bell, a bargain picked up in the course of preparations, woke the neighborhood. Its message was simple: the first Discalced Carmelite monastery was no longer a plan. It was a reality.

It was all very simple and unassuming. Gaspar Daza, representing the bishop, gave the habit to the first four nuns. Only close friends were present—those who had fought the good fight together.

That was by no means the end of the opposition, trials, and tribulations that the nuns had come through. But what was to follow had an effect similar to that of snow and ice on the grain of wheat; it helped the undertaking to put down deep roots for a future fruitful harvest.

As a contribution to this process, the city council kept up a never-ending lawsuit over some alleged wells. Mother Teresa was summoned back to the Incarnation, tried for her crime, and threatened with monastic imprisonment. And to make matters worse, word of these happenings was beginning to cause a stir at the courts of Madrid and Rome.

But in time the storm subsided and Teresa returned to her little dovecote, as she liked to call St. Joseph's, with her title to foundress well and truly established.

Since then St. Joseph's and everything in it speaks to us of St. Teresa. Every corner of the house bears the stamp of her spirit. We cannot see her, but we feel her presence. We cannot touch her, but we are continually touching objects she used, rooms she lived in.

Next to the monastery, deliberately small "so that it wouldn't make much noise when it fell on Judgment Day" (WP 2.9), and beside the church that was built at the beginning of the 17th century, is *St. Paul's Chapel*. God told Moses to remove his sandals, that the ground he walked on was holy. That is what one feels on entering this entranceway to places hallowed by St. Teresa: the urge to strip ourselves of nonessentials, as the first Discalced Carmelite nuns did before this altar.

Inner cloister of the Carmel of St. Joseph

St. Paul's Chapel was built by Francisco de Salcedo, a noted benefactor of St. Teresa, who is buried here.

Several other friends and relatives of St. Teresa are interred in the adjacent magnificent **monastery Church of San José and its Chapels.** Among them (in the apse): Don Álvaro de Mendoza (+1586); in the Chapel of St. John of the Cross, Gaspar Daza (+1592) and his mother and sister. Here too rests Teresa's faithful chaplain, Julian of Ávila (+1605).

In the Chapel of St. Lawrence we find the tombs of St. Teresa's brothers Lorenzo de Cepeda (+1580) and Pedro de Ahumada (+1589), an uncle and his wife, a nephew, and other relatives and friends.

From the ornate church we move to the simplicity of the monastery itself.

The heart of the house is the saint's *cell.* Simple, clean, with only a wooden bed for furniture and a cork mat for carpet. It is the typical environment of someone determined not to be held back by the things of this world and whose only desire is to be "alone with Him alone." And there to the left, under the window that, according to Teresa, if shut she couldn't see and if opened she froze, is her teaching podium. That rough stone ledge was the desk on which, seated on the floor, she wrote her *Life*—that masterpiece similar to St. Augustine's *Confessions,* in which she sings of God's many mercies toward her. Here too she wrote the first version of the *Way of Perfection.* Looking ahead in time, we might think of it as the inaugural lecture of one who was destined to be declared a Doctor of the Church and mother of God-seekers everywhere.

We move on now to the *chapter room.* The outstanding feature here is her *prioress's seat,* her "other pulpit." No greater tribute can be paid her than to say that whatever difference there is between this simple chair and those elaborate thrones used by the abbesses of her time was no coincidence; it was quite deliberate.

The *recreation room* was another key place in Teresa's new style of monastic living. Naturally, it was based on friendship with God, on work, poverty, and self-denial; but Teresa also brought to it those elements of

The small bell from St. Teresa's first foundation, now at St. Joseph's

"The Devil's Staircase"

The saint's cell in the Carmel of St. Joseph in Ávila. At left, the stone ledge on which she wrote her *Life*, *The Way of Perfection*, and *The Interior Castle*

simple, friendly, cheerful, and even fun-loving community relationships typical of one who had no time for "long-faced saints."

And let's not forget the ***kitchen***, a place where Teresa once gave the comforting reminder that God was as present "among the pots and pans" as he was anywhere else.

Just another step and we're in the ***garden***, at once the lungs and larder of the community, a window onto that little bit of clear Castilian sky, so transparent that we can sense God beyond.

On one side of the garden is the ***Samaritan woman's well***, named after one of Teresa's favorite Scripture passages. In the other part of the garden are her beloved hermitages. Built with materials from an old dovecote, the ***hermitages*** are named in honor of Nazareth, Christ the Lord, St. Augustine, and St. Catherine. In these humble little buildings Teresa's nuns, like the fathers of the desert, sought even greater solitude to better immerse themselves in the Divine.

"Christ of the beautiful eyes," in its hermitage in the garden of St. Joseph, Ávila

There are so many interesting memories here that the list could go on endlessly: *the devil's staircase* (so-called because Teresa tumbled down them on Christmas Eve 1577 and broke her left arm); paintings like the one called "*Christ of the Beautiful Eyes*"; the *mule chair saddle* she once rode on; and so much more. Everything here speaks of her, but St. Joseph's is not the only place to do so.

It is unfortunate in a way that this book is intended only as a guide to places founded by St. Teresa. But it would be impossible to look only at her destinations and forget where she started from: the *Monastery of the Incarnation.*

Teresa knocked on its doors on November 2, 1533. She had just been through a serious illness and looked upon entry here as building her tomb. It turned out instead to be the cradle of her virtues, the nursery from which several of her Discalced nuns were transplanted. The twenty-nine years she spent there left her with grateful and affectionate memories, surprising perhaps for a place she was eventually destined to leave in order to find her true vocation. The Incarnation is full of Teresian atmosphere: parlors, oratory, stairs, books, paintings, and so many other objects tell us she has been here.

And the city itself? Its famous walls encase a veritable treasure chest, and the reader can admire these in the illustrations: the *Carmen Gate; Our Lady of Charity; "La Santa," the house where St. Teresa was born; the convent of Our Lady of Grace*, and so many other places.

On the following page:
The church of Carmel of St. Joseph, Ávila,
with the statue of St. Joseph enshrined above
the high altar

MEDINA Teresian Events and Dates

1560
August

Fray Alonso Maldonado, Franciscan missionary in Mexico, fires Teresa with zeal; millions of native peoples have not heard the Gospel.

1567
February

Juan Bautista Rubeo, general of the Carmelite Order, arrives in Ávila and meets Teresa at St. Joseph's.

April 27

The father general authorizes Mother Teresa to found new Carmels in Castile.

June–July

Teresa requests the general's authorization to found monasteries of Carmelite friars.

Summer

Fray John of the Cross—at the time still known as John of St. Matthias—a student at Salamanca recently ordained a priest, goes to Medina where he offers his first Mass.

August 10

The father general authorizes Teresa to found two monasteries of Carmelite friars in Castile.

August 13

With her group of nuns, Teresa sets out from Ávila for Medina del Campo. They spend the night (13–14) at Arévalo.

August 15

Teresa founds the Carmel of Medina.

August 16

The general authorizes Teresa to found monasteries of Carmelite friars.

Contemporary Events

1566

The Dominican Michael Ghislieri is elected pope. As Pope Pius V he enacts the reforms of the Council of Trent.

1567
April 16

Pius V entrusts the reform of religious orders to the bishops.

September

On orders of King Philip II, Fernando Álvarez de Toledo, the Duke of Alba, reaches the Spanish Netherlands with an army of mercenaries to restore order in the region. His "Council of Troubles" (or Council of Blood) punishes ringleaders of political and religious unrest there. In seven years, almost 9,000 people are convicted of heresy or treason; more than 1,000 are executed, and more than 60,000 are arrested and exiled.

The Book of the Foundations, beginning of the autograph relating to the foundation of Medina: "Chapter III: how plans began to be made for the foundation of the monastery of St. Joseph's in Medina del Campo."

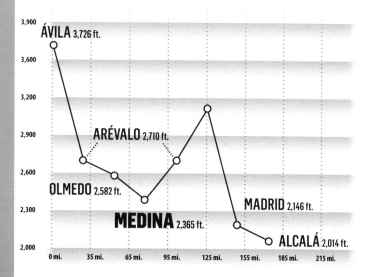

Chart of St. Teresa's travels in 1567 the Medina foundation

Medina del Campo

ST. JOSEPH'S MONASTERY

AUGUST 15, 1567

Once the storms that surrounded the early days of St. Joseph's, Ávila, had passed, it was a little haven of peace and grace. For Teresa the next five years during which she was prioress were "the most restful in her life" (F 1.1). With the thirteen nuns, which were the most she would take at that time (later she allowed twenty-one), "she was enjoying herself with people who were so holy and pure that their only thought was for the praise and service of God" (F 1.2).

Exterior of the Medina monastery; drawing by the Belgian artist Hye Hoys (1866)

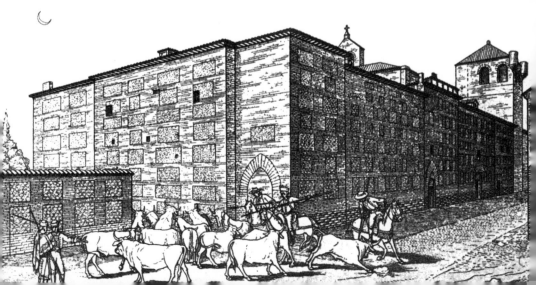

But pleasures, however pure, were not this woman's nourishment. Teresa could no more contain the volcanic expansion of love within her than we could hold air in our fist. One day a Franciscan missionary in Mexico, Alonso de Maldonado, happened to visit the community and proceeded to tell Teresa about the multitude of souls being lost in the Americas, or the Indies, as they were then known.

Shortly afterward came the first, and unexpected, visit from the Carmelite prior general, Father Juan Bautista Rubeo (or Rossi). For Teresa, it might have been a dreaded visit, because he could have been angry with her for leaving the Incarnation and transferring her obedience to the bishop. Instead, what he saw there so thrilled him that he gave her complete freedom to make further foundations.

In Teresa's mind, it was all one thing: to be able to make new foundations, to want to do so in order that through prayer fewer souls would be lost, and to be on the lookout for her next conquest. And the place that came to mind immediately was Medina del Campo.

There were various reasons for her choice: It was nearby—just two days' mule ride. She knew an influential man there, who was ready to help: Father Baltasar Álvarez, the Jesuit rector and her onetime confessor. The Carmelite prior, Father Antonio de Heredia, was also well disposed to the idea and knew a woman who would sell them a house. Besides, Medina itself was quite a cosmopolitan commercial center, well known both in Europe and the Americas; it had a touch of universality.

This latter aspect, however, was also a complicating factor. A proud city that engraved a motto such as "No Office for the King, No Benefice for the Pope" on its coat of arms was unlikely to welcome such a foundation. But Teresa's friends got to work; the clergy, nobility, and city fathers gave unanimous approval. All was arranged. Mother Teresa was informed that she could come whenever she liked.

No sooner said than done. With a little borrowed money for capital, "two nuns from St. Joseph's and myself, with four from the Incarnation, left Ávila . . . with our chaplain, Father Julian de Ávila" (F 3.2). This was their first founding expedition, and it had an air of adventure, exploration,

Left and center: Upper cloister and courtyard of the Medina Carmel

and conquest about it. Notwithstanding much advice to the contrary, the little party set off in the full light of day, as if to put the humiliations suffered on the occasion of their taking possession of St. Joseph's behind them for good.

That was August 13, 1567. They passed through Cardeñosa and Gotarrendura, full of childhood memories for Teresa, and stopped at Arévalo to spend the night with "some devout ladies" (F 3.2).

Either the devil had been sleeping and now suddenly woke up, or God doesn't allow his works to be accomplished without problems. However one looks at it, problems lay in wait.

Word came from Medina that the Augustinians had raised objections about the house the nuns had rented. The nuns, already in Arévalo, were instructed not to leave Ávila! The faithful Father Julian summed up how they felt: "When I heard this and remembered the fanfare with which we left Ávila, I thought of the laughter and mockery that would greet our return. . . . It upset me quite a lot" (*Vida* II).

Teresa, the nuns, and Father Julian spent the night planning and making decisions rather than sleeping. The final decision was to go on to Medina

The Mount Carmel hermitage in the monastery garden

and stay in the house that Father Antonio had been trying to buy, no matter what state it was in.

So after a detour to visit the bishop of Ávila at Olmedo, the party reached Medina after nightfall. They stopped at the Carmelite priory and decided to go the rest of the way on foot so as not to attract attention. One problem: They forgot that this was the very night when the bulls were being penned for the following day's bullfight!

Let's listen to Julian's account: "We took the vestments and other things necessary for saying Mass [from the Carmelite priory] and, without more ado, set off on foot—nuns, clergy, the prior and two or three friars— taking a roundabout way to avoid the bulls, which were being penned just then. . . . We were all loaded down and looked like a party of gypsies who had just robbed a church. Certainly, if we had met any police they would have had to take us to jail until they found out where priests, friars, and nuns were going at that hour of the night" (*Vida*).

They eventually reached the house, armed with a letter from its owner requesting the caretaker to assist them. But what a night lay in store for them! When the caretaker and his wife had been roused, they insisted on summoning a notary right then and there to record all the events of the night. Meanwhile, Teresa and her friends cleared the entranceway of rubbish, cleaned it up, and decorated the crumbling walls with a few hangings. At last an altar was ready, someone rang a bell, the Carmelite prior said Mass, and the Blessed Sacrament was reserved.

Teresa was delighted with herself: "To see another church where the Blessed Sacrament was reserved was always one of my greatest comforts," she said (F 3.10). That was fine in the dark, but then the full light of the Castilian sun on August 15 revealed the real situation. Suddenly Teresa's joy over one tabernacle more became acute anxiety that she might soon have one tabernacle less!

Her delight, then, was short-lived, "because after Mass I looked out of the window at the inner courtyard only to find that the walls had actually fallen in places. . . . When I realized that His Majesty had been placed on the side of the street in the dangerous times we live in because of those Lutherans, how my heart was troubled!" (F 3.10).

Nevertheless, there they had to stay for another week, when a local merchant offered Teresa the upper story of his house until her own was fit to live in. That took another two months. Later, through the generosity of Doña Elena de Quiroga (who became a nun herself in 1581), a lovely little church was added to the building, thus completing the foundation.

There are still a few points to touch on in this hurried account of the Medina foundation. The first is to fill the reader in a little on that devotion to the Eucharist we saw evidence of in Teresa's enthusiasm over one more tabernacle. She actually had a guard posted to watch it every night—and even got up to check that the watchmen were awake.

Like every believer, Teresa was aware that the God we worship is one who wants to communicate with us. But she also knew that he tends to disguise this communication—in a burning bush, in wind, in human beings. She was in love with God-made-man but was aware that since his ascension into heaven Christ could be found body and blood, soul and divinity, only in the Eucharist, celebrated and reserved. "The Lord had given her such strong faith that when she heard people saying they would like to have been alive when Jesus was on earth, she used to laugh to herself because she regarded Him as being just as much present in the Blessed Sacrament as He had been then; so what difference did it make to them?" (WP 34.6). Perhaps that is why she received her greatest graces after Communion, and why she insisted with her daughters, "Stay with Him willingly. Don't lose so good an opportunity for your communication with Him as the time after Communion affords you" (WP 34.12).

Medina holds major significance in Teresa's life for another reason. It was here that she first met Fray John of the Cross, the man destined to be the first Discalced Carmelite friar, a saint, mystical poet, and Doctor of the Church.

Teresa had often thought about how good it would be if her Discalced Order also had a male branch to minister to the spiritual needs of her nuns. After getting permission she discussed the idea with Father Antonio de Heredia, who to her surprise offered to be the first. Then one day "a young father happened to come there . . . whose name was Father John of the Cross [at the time still known by his name as a Calced Carmelite, John of St. Matthias]. I praised the Lord and, having spoken with him, was very pleased with him. He told me that he too (like Father Antonio) wanted to go and join the Carthusians. I explained what I had in mind and pressed him to wait until the Lord gave us a monastery. I emphasized how good it would be if he could perfect himself in his own Order. . . . He promised to wait, provided he didn't have to wait too long" (F 3.17). He didn't have long to wait, but we'll return to that later.

Here then is the Medina Carmel, snug in the shadow of the Castillo de la Mota, a castle that would seem to protect Teresa's footprints from the shifting sands of time. Here you can see such signs of her presence as her *breviary,* the *embroidery* with which she illustrated biblical passages in gold and silver on vestments, her *account ledger,* and other objects and places in the monastery that are particularly associated with her. Yet these things are but a shadow of the most precious thing she left behind: her spirit is as much alive there today as when she sat in this convent writing her *Book of the Foundations.*

The Book of the Foundations, which narrates the beginning of the journey to Malagón: "Chapter IX: treats of how she left Medina del Campo for the foundation of St. Joseph's at Malagón."

MALAGÓN
Dates and Events concerning Teresa's Third Foundation

1568
January–February

Teresa travels from Medina del Campo to Alcalá de Henares. She advises María de Jesus and organizes the Carmel of Alcalá that Maria has founded. Teresa makes a brief stop in Madrid.

March

The saint leaves Alcalá and reaches Toledo. On March 30, in Doña Luisa de la Cerda's palace, she signs the documents for the foundation of her third Carmel, Malagón.

March 31

Teresa sets out for Malagón. The little house for the new Carmel is inaugurated on April 11.

April

Teresa entrusts the manuscript of the book of her *Life* to Doña Luisa de la Cerda and asks her to deliver it to St. John of Ávila in Montilla (Córdoba).

May–June

Teresa writes a series of letters (at least four to Doña Luisa, reminding

her of her promise to deliver the *Life* to John of Ávila).

May 19

Teresa leaves Malagón for Ávila, where she spends almost all the month of June. In mid-May she still has no word if her *Life* has reached its destination.

June 30

Another trip, this time from Ávila to Medina. On the way she visits the farm at Duruelo, later to be St. John of the Cross's monastery.

Early July

In Medina, an interior voice urges her to found the Valladolid Carmel.

July 6

John of the Cross delivers letters to Ávila to negotiate the Duruelo foundation.

August 9

Accompanied by John of the Cross, Teresa sets out from Medina for Valladolid.

September 12

St. John of Ávila writes to Mother Teresa expressing his approval of the book of her *Life*.

**1569
May 10**

John of Ávila dies at Montilla.

An Important Development

Teresa's first book is approved by the great master of the spirituals, St. John of Ávila. For Teresa, this book is "her whole soul" and represents her enormous effort to express all that has happened in her life. The positive response from the "Apostle of Andalusia" clears away the cloud of anxiety and doubt that has troubled Teresa for years. She sees this approval as the voice of the church corroborating her prophetic charism, her vocation as a writer, and her experience of God.

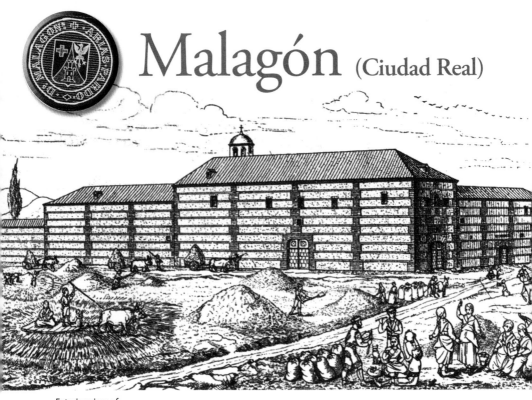

Malagón (Ciudad Real)

Exterior view of the Carmel of Malagón; drawing by Hye Hoys (1866–1867)

ST. JOSEPH'S MONASTERY

APRIL 11, 1568

The events described in the last chapter have brought us to about October 1567. Mother Teresa of Jesus is consoled, praising the Lord that her Medina nuns "are following in the footsteps of those at St. Joseph's, Ávila" (F 9.1).

Teresa's good friend Doña Luisa de la Cerda, sister of the Duke of Medinaceli, is the woman in Toledo whom Teresa had been sent to console on her husband's death. She now learned something that was about to give Teresa another change of scene. Having discovered that Teresa had been given permission to make additional foundations, Doña Luisa thought it would be a good idea to get her to found a monastery in honor of her late husband in the very city where he had ruled: Malagón.

Referring to Doña Luisa, Teresa wrote,

> She began to pester me . . . I wanted none of it, because the place was so small that some sort of endowment would have to be arranged and that was something to which I was very much opposed. . . . I discussed it with learned men and with my confessor, and they told me I was wrong. The Council [of Trent] had permitted this, they said, and a monastery in which the Lord could be served so well should not be dropped in favor of my opinion. With this and the lady's continuing insistence I had no choice but to give in. She gave an adequate endowment, because I like the monasteries to be either completely poor or so provided for that the nuns do not have to bother anybody for what they need. (F 9.2–3)

So Teresa is about to learn another lesson in that difficult course from which she would graduate with the title "God's wandering woman." Accompanied by Ana de los Angeles, who was to be prioress of the new community, she set out from Medina. A stopover at St. Joseph's, Ávila, to pick up another nun for the undertaking, was a joy for all concerned. It was Teresa's first return to the monastery that she thought of as "hers" in a special way. But the journey ahead was long, so the visit had to be cut short. The first part of the trip took them over the mountains. Then two weeks' rest at the home of Doña Leonor de Mascareñas, onetime governess to King Philip II, in Madrid, and on once more toward Alcalá.

They entered the city by the Madrid Gate and stopped a little way in on the right-hand side. Here a difficult task awaited the foundress: she had to temper the rigorous observance of a community that the Venerable María de Jesus had founded there, much along the same lines as Ávila and Medina. Teresa had met this Andalusian widow, who had journeyed barefoot to

Rome to obtain permission to found her Discalced Carmelite monastery, at Doña Luisa's palace in Toledo. Since their objectives were similar, they had a lot to talk about and quickly became friends. And according to St. Teresa, it was this woman who could neither read nor write who taught her "what with all her reading of the Constitutions" she had not noticed, namely, that the Rule she was seeking to live by forbade property and endowments. This was a detail that strongly influenced the style of Teresa's reform and caused her no few headaches along the way.

It was now Teresa's turn to return the favor. At María's own request, Teresa proceeded to remove from this monastery everything that had turned it into an arena of mortification—a veritable hairshirt market!—and to turn it into one of the simplest and most cheerful of her dovecotes.

That took her two months, and then it was on to Toledo, where they stayed with Doña Luisa in her palace overlooking the city. It was her first visit since the days when preparations for Ávila were just beginning, so memories came flooding back: memories of God, for it was here that she had written her *Life*; her memories of the loving attentiveness of Doña Luisa; and memories of her conversations with the servants, from whose midst she obtained that sterling vocation, María de San José (Salazar). Here she could reminisce and finalize the details of the foundation on which she had embarked. That done, and having summoned four more nuns from the Incarnation at Ávila, Teresa set out for Malagón. She was accompanied by Doña Luisa, with some of her servants, and a ponderous Jesuit whom Teresa mischievously nicknamed "the Eternal Father." Fifty-two miles lay ahead: rough, sometimes mountainous country but traveled with a little less difficulty than expected, thanks to Doña Luisa's knowledge of the countryside. Finally, on April 1, they arrived, and in no time had every able-bodied person in the village organized to help them. As usual, the house was not yet ready for occupation, so they stayed in Doña Luisa's imposing castle for the time being.

On April 11, "Palm Sunday, a procession of townsfolk came to accompany us, and, with lowered veils and white mantles, we proceeded

Church of
St. Mary Major
in Daimiel

Malagón, monument to the saint

to the parish church. There a sermon was preached and then the Blessed Sacrament was borne to our monastery" (F 9.5).

Before long they discovered one big mistake that had been made: the house was very close to the noisy city market. Mother Teresa was immediately allowed to choose a better site and was even offered one at the north end of the town. But she refused it in favor of one on the south side, saying the other was destined for a Franciscan monastery. And she proved to be right: some time afterward the sons of her protector, St. Peter of Alcántara, came to settle there. According to tradition, Teresa saw a beautiful white dove perched on an olive tree south of the town and chose that site for her definitive foundation there.

Doña Luisa gave Teresa complete freedom in the design, building, and furnishings of this monastery. The original accounts and other documentation concerning it are still in the convent safe to prove it. Work began immediately, but it was eleven years before Teresa could return for the solemn transfer from old monastery to new. She may of course have visited it in the meantime, while on one of her trips, for she certainly enlisted nuns from Malagón for subsequent foundations.

Anne of St. Bartholomew, Teresa's faithful companion, describes the foundress's arrival in Malagón on November 25, 1579: "After a dreadful journey and several bad nights, she arrived so ill that every bone in her body ached and she was unfit to leave her bed." But a woman of Teresa's energy is difficult to keep in bed. As soon as the construction workers

Views of the upper and lower cloister and courtyard, Carmel of Malagón

reported that the work would take about another six months, she was up at dawn the following day to see for herself. She inspected what had been done, made her calculations regarding the remainder, and announced that it was to be ready for the feast of the Immaculate Conception—just twelve days away!

Leaving masons, carpenters, and friends to recover from that shock as best they could, she went on-site from morning til night—skipping meals, rest, and even prayer time. And when she was not lending a hand herself,

Water filter

Niche with the saint's podium, across from the
Carmel of Malagón

she directed operations from a stone "podium," which is still preserved to
this day. Needless to say, the builders met her deadline!

We cannot end our account of the Malagón foundation without mentioning some of the features that distinguished it from the rest.

In the first place, it was the only monastery that the foundress herself built from scratch. Elsewhere, conditions about the place, shortage
of money, or remodeling of existing buildings all had a restricting influence. This building expresses fully what Teresa thought was suitable for her
nuns—the type of building, the layout, and the space required.

Communion window

For that reason, St. Joseph's at Malagón is a real relic, and the nuns go to great pains to keep it absolutely unchanged. Even repairs are made with the original materials. No wonder "the plans" have been requested from all over the world for new Carmels.

Another point about this third foundation is the way it illustrates the astounding flexibility of spirit that enabled Teresa to adapt her ideal of a reformed Carmel to varying circumstances.

We sometimes take as "fidelity to the spirit," to "the primitive ideal," or to "the charism" what in reality is only spiritual narrowness, inertia, or simply the convenient repetition of rules—something that is much easier to do than to constantly adapt them to the needs of the moment.

When she was founding St. Joseph's in Ávila, Teresa defended tooth and nail her ideal—based on the primitive Rule—of a radically poor house, without money or endowment. Yet, here she accepts the latter for the reasons we have mentioned.

In this Castilian hinterland, the nuns would have difficulty finding fish, thus making it a challenge to observe abstinence from meat, which seemed such an important part of the Rule. But Teresa agreed to go ahead with this foundation anyway.

And then there was the contemplative life itself. To be "alone with God alone" was "the reason the Lord had brought them together there." But when Teresa realized the grave economic needs of the townspeople, she had her nuns finance a sewing workshop for the girls and paid a priest and an assistant to teach the boys. "What other alms but this can we give?" she asked.

Finally, another new, though not original, element: it was here that she first admitted "lay sisters." These were nuns who undertook the manual work in the house; they were not obliged to the recitation of the Divine Office as were the choir nuns. By shouldering other work duties the lay sisters greatly facilitated the heavy liturgical commitment of the rest of the community.

Let no one think, however, that such modifications here and in some subsequent foundations meant these were in any way inferior. No, indeed. And lest such an idea should occur to anyone, including Teresa, Jesus himself assured her "that He would be well served in that house" (F 9.5).

One last point, to honor the people who first made this Carmel possible and who have so lovingly supported it to this day, let us state one simple fact: if Teresa of Jesus is the saint of a place called Ávila, Malagón is undoubtedly the place of a saint called Teresa of Jesus.

The love of the people of Malagón for St. Teresa and her daughters is proverbial. And the shrine in the little square leading to the monastery and

The monastery's original turn

church is a symbol of it. There, framed for posterity, is a likeness of the saint and the famous stone on which she used to rest while directing the building work. The townsfolk testify to their devotion with a perpetually burning oil lamp, plenty of electric lights all year round, and an abundance of fresh flowers. They never pass their little shrine without making some sign of faith and devotion.

44

Autograph of *The Book of the Foundations,* beginning of the foundation of the monastery at Duruelo: "Chapter thirteen: treats of how and by whom the first monastery of the primitive Rule was founded for discalced friars, in the year MDLXVIII. — Before I went to this foundation in Valladolid, as had already been arranged with Padre Antonio . . ."

VALLADOLID
St. Teresa's Route from Toledo to Valladolid

1568
Late May
Teresa leaves Toledo for Escalona.

June 2
She arrives in Ávila and stays there until the end of the month.

June 30
Teresa leaves Ávila for Medina, making a detour to visit the farm at Duruelo.

July 1
She arrives in Medina del Campo.

August 10
After traveling from Medina with John of the Cross, Teresa and John reach Valladolid.

August 15
The new monastery at Valladolid is established at Río de Olmos, on the banks of the river Pisuerga.

4,600

DURUELO 4,242 ft.

4,000

ÁVILA 3,726 ft.

MALAGÓN 2,080 ft.

3,300

ALBA 2,740 ft.

MADRID 2,146 ft.

2,600

VALLADOLID 2,270 ft.

MEDINA 2,365 ft.

2,000

ALCALÁ 2,014 ft.

TOLEDO 1,736 ft.

ESCALONA 1509 ft.

1,300

0 mi.   60 mi.   120 mi.   180 mi.   240 mi.   300 mi.   370 mi.   430 mi

1568

Chart of St. Teresa's travels in 1568
the Valladolid foundation

September 30

Teresa bids farewell to John of the Cross, who leaves for Duruelo.

November 28

John of the Cross and Antonio de Heredia set up the new Carmelite monastery for friars at the little house in Duruelo.

An Important Event

Father John of the Cross receives training and formation in Discalced Carmelite life from Mother Teresa herself. She is 53 years old, he's 26. The two are profoundly different, but they share the mystical vocation and the depth of their experience of God. John is willingly trained in the lifestyle, family spirit, spirit of prayer, and recreation that Teresa has instilled in the new little group.

Valladolid

MONASTERY OF THE CONCEPTION OF OUR LADY OF MOUNT CARMEL

AUGUST 15, 1568

St. Teresa tells the story of this foundation in chapter 10 of her *Book of the Foundations:*

Exterior view of the Valladolid monastery; drawing by Hye Hoys (1866–1867)

> Four or five months before I founded the Malagón monastery, I was talking to an important gentleman [Don Bernardino de Mendoza, brother of the bishop of Ávila] and he told me that if I wanted to make a foundation in Valladolid, he would give a house he had there, with a fine big garden. Though I was not eager about it as a place for a foundation, because it was almost a quarter of a league from the town, I accepted. . . .

Two months later, this young man was laid low by a sudden illness which deprived him of the power of speech. He could scarcely make his confession, though he did make many signs to indicate that he was asking God's forgiveness. Shortly afterwards he died. The Lord told me that his salvation had been very much at risk, but that He had had mercy on him because of the favor he did His Mother in giving that house as a monastery of her Order. He would not leave purgatory, however, until the first Mass had been said in that house. I was so conscious of the grave sufferings of that soul that, though I wanted to found in Toledo, I left that aside for the moment and tried to found as quickly as possible in Valladolid instead.

A look at the calendar lets us witness Teresa's haste. Having made provisional arrangements for her nuns, she left Malagón on May 19, 1568. On May 29, she left Toledo for Escalona and spent June in Ávila, where she arrived "rather tired." Teresa was still prioress of Ávila and could not leave it as quickly as she might have liked; the absence just past and that which she was preparing for meant that a lot of details had to be attended to so that the community could carry on without her.

Setting out again on June 30, she reached Medina after losing a lot of time looking for a little place called Duruelo—of which we'll say more later. Now she encountered another delay for community business and matters relating to her desire, fast becoming an obsession, to found a house of Discalced Carmelite friars. In the midst of her preoccupation with this dream, the Lord gave her a reminder about Valladolid: "While I was praying one day, He told me to hurry: that that soul was suffering a lot" (F 10.3).

So it was back on the road again, and quickly to her destination: Río Olmos, a mile and a half or so from Valladolid. With her were three nuns from Ávila, three from Medina, a postulant, and Father John of the Cross. The man who was to be her first Discalced friar was having his first outing with his sisters and chatting with them about God and the new lifestyle he was to copy from them.

Once they reached Valladolid, reality set in. Teresa writes, "As soon as I saw the house I was quite distressed, because I realized that it would be foolish to expect nuns to live there. The beautiful garden made it very pleasant, but it couldn't be healthy so near the river" (F 10.3). Nevertheless, she quickly got on with the necessary adjustments. Everything was done with the utmost secrecy, for Father Julian, her faithful chaplain, had not yet obtained the permission of the ecclesiastical authorities for the foundation.

In the midst of all this, who should pay them an unexpected visit but the vicar general of the city. He must have been impressed, because he immediately allowed them to have Mass celebrated and promised to expedite the permission they were looking for.

"Little did I think that what had been said to me about that gentleman would be fulfilled just then. . . . But when the priest approached us with the Host at Communion time, just as I was about to receive it I had a vision of the said gentleman beside the priest, his face resplendent and full of joy. . . . He thanked me for what I had done to enable him to leave purgatory and go to heaven" (F 10.5).

The official opening took place that same week: August 15, the feast of the Assumption of the Blessed Virgin Mary.

It was not long before St. Teresa's misgivings about the healthiness of the place began to be justified. Beautiful though its setting was between the Pisuerga and Olmos rivers, always fresh and green behind screens of poplar trees, it was nevertheless extremely damp and unhealthy. Soon, all the sisters had been laid low by malaria. As long as she could stay on her feet Mother Teresa served and fed them all, made their beds and nursed them. It became only too obvious that they would have to move elsewhere.

Doña María de Mendoza, a sister both of their late benefactor and of the bishop of Ávila, undertook to find them another site. The agreement was that in return for Río Olmos she would find them a place on the outskirts of the city, near the main road leading from St. Clare's Gate. The property she had in mind, however, belonged to an entailed estate, and negotiations for its purchase were slow. Meanwhile, the great-hearted Doña María brought the community to her own house, where "she killed them with kindness," and there they spent Christmas. It was there that on Christmas Eve St. Teresa "gave a talk the like of which they had never heard before." According to the chronicler of this event, "She spoke of the Infant's tears, the mother's

Valladolid; upper cloister of the National Museum of Sculpture

poverty, the hardness of the crib, the severity of the weather and the uncomfortableness of the stable. Such was the spirit and fervor with which she spoke that everyone went away comforted and happy, ready and willing to face the challenge of any hardship."

The new monastery was eventually ready for occupation on February 3, the feast of St. Blaise. The bishop of Ávila attended with all the clergy of the city, both secular and religious. Nobility and grandees turned out in force. The streets were bedecked with bunting; lights and perfumed candles burned along the way. By all accounts, it was quite a procession. And all eyes were on Mother Teresa, who by now was beginning to be looked upon as a saint.

So much for the facts of the foundation. But there are some other things worth mentioning here too. First of all, the community. Doña María de Ocampo, that niece of Teresa's who first suggested reforming the Carmelite life in one of their little get-togethers at the Incarnation, became Sister María Bautista and prioress of this monastery. Here too lived Casilda de Padilla, the nun who so impressed Teresa that she devoted nearly two chapters of the *Book of the Foundations* to a moving account of her exemplary life, so that the memory of it should never die.

In fact, in the 16th and 17th centuries, the Valladolid monastery produced a whole generation of humanist nuns. They read Latin, Greek, and Hebrew; they were well versed in the Scriptures. Many were noteworthy poets, especially Cecilia del Nacimiento, who could be compared to the great Spanish writers Lope de Vega and Francisco de Quevedo.

This monastery is also the proud repository of some of St. Teresa's writings. She wrote her *Way of Perfection* twice; the second version is in this monastery. The community treasures with equal love the greatest single holding of her letters—over fifty in all. Looking at them, one cannot help thinking how much greater St. Teresa's literary and doctrinal legacy would be if only all the communities of friars and nuns had been as careful to keep all her letters as this one was.

The last point we would like to consider brings us back to the beginning of this account of the Valladolid foundation. We mentioned the detour that

View of Duruelo

Courtyard at the monastery entrance

St. Teresa's party made in search of a little place called Duruelo, a place she was to visit again on her way to Toledo. What was the attraction of such an out-of-the-way little hamlet? It was here that Teresa's dream of extending her reform to the Carmelite friars had just come true. When speaking of the Medina foundation, we mentioned the agreement that Teresa made with Fathers Antonio de Heredia and John of the Cross (or John of St. Matthias as he was then known): her promise not to keep them waiting. The best she could do in the short term was to accept the offer of a tumbledown shack in Duruelo from a certain Don Rafael of Ávila. After laborious negotiations, she obtained the permission of the male branch of the Carmelite Order for a new expression of their life. It was begun in Duruelo on November 28, 1568, with the two fathers mentioned—henceforth known as Anthony of Jesus and John of the Cross—as the first Discalced friars' community.

Speaking of the extreme poverty of this house, Teresa wrote, "It didn't take long to get the house ready because, although they would have liked to do more, there just wasn't any money." She was deeply moved by what she saw: "I shall never forget a little wooden cross they had over the holy water

St. Teresa's hermitage in the monastery garden

Original hand-written copy of *The Way of Perfection* in a silver case, and a facsimile of the text

font. It had a little paper picture of Christ stuck to it, and I found it more devotional than if it had been really well made" (F 14.2 and 7).

What did Teresa expect of her Discalced friars? Surely, to maintain and communicate all she had discovered and experienced herself. What Teresa had discovered was a new image of the heavenly Father. She saw him as a friend, in the midst of human affairs, so near that he walked, as she wrote, among the pots and pans; hidden within the castle of each person's soul, he was so easily approachable that she described prayer as the conversation between friends.

In Christ, Teresa discovered the Master, the living Book, God adapted to the measure of her woman's heart, the Spouse whose honor is hers just as hers is his.

Teresa discovered the church in all the glory of its dignity as bride of Christ but, nevertheless, "beset by great evils." She did not clamor against hierarchies or faulty structures; she was content to be a faithful and obedient daughter, and to see to it that her daughters at least would be the same. In this warfare she found a powerful and definitive weapon: for the good of the church she created a new style of monastic life, communities that would be

Antique alabaster statue of the Blessed Virgin and Child, venerated in the Valladolid monastery

On the following page:
Statue of St. Teresa, school of Gregorio Fernández

"little colleges of Christ." Teresa had a clear vision for these select groups: they would be few in number, living in poverty and thirsting for depth. They would be conspicuous for the simplicity of their lives, their contagious cheerfulness, and their constant prayer for the defenders of the church. In a word, they would be the light, salt, and leaven that the world needed.

Teresa felt herself to be, as she said, "only a weak and worthless woman." For that reason she wanted a male branch of Discalced Carmel. These men, with their experience of God, their learning, and knowledge of the nuns' lifestyle, would make the reformed Carmel complete. The friars would teach, encourage, and watch over the nuns as brothers do. Besides, the friars, with fewer restrictions than women, could and would set forth to the foreign missions to bring more souls to the light of the Gospel.

God rewarded Teresa with a very rare gift: the personification of all her dreams in the humble person of the first Discalced Carmelite friar, Father John of the Cross. When she spoke with him through the parlor grilles in Medina and Valladolid, taught him her ways, and made his first habit for him, she found him to be a refined, open, and learned man in search of a very specific vocation. That won her heart completely.

John of the Cross was a prayerful man and a lover of solitude. He could capture beauty in poetry with the best. He loved his Order. But above all, he was open to the new "family style" life created by Teresa and had no reluctance to learn about it from a group of women who were already living it.

The chief thing that made Teresa so enthusiastic about John of the Cross, however, was his experience of God. Rarely in history have two people met who were so immersed in the mystery of God, so capable of savoring it, of expressing it in poetry and prose, and above all, of spreading it about them.

John of the Cross was the embodiment of all the teaching, advice, and guidelines that Teresa imparted to the friars. Because of what she gave them through him and because of what she suffered that they might come into being, the friars have always regarded her as their foundress . . . and mother.

TOLEDO
St. Teresa's Route from Valladolid to Toledo

1568
December

From Valladolid Teresa arranges for the foundation of the Carmel at Toledo. An exchange of letters with Father Pablo Hernández and the founders.

1569
February 22

Teresa begins the trip from Valladolid to Medina and Duruelo; she stays two weeks at St. Joseph's, Ávila.

March 24

Teresa arrives in Toledo. Problems! The ecclesiastical governor's authorization to establish the foundation isn't granted until May 8.

May 14

The saint establishes the Toledo Carmel, her fifth foundation.

May 30

More travels, this time from Toledo to Pastrana, via the imperial court.

Important Background

Mother Teresa already knows Toledo. She is familiar with the city's imperial splendor, its palaces and nobility. Now she gets a firsthand look at the tragedy afflicting this major see. Its archbishop, the Dominican Bartolomé de Carranza—a very spiritual man, a good writer, friend of Father Luis de Granada, and also probably a kindred soul of Mother Teresa—has been in various prisons since 1559. The Church of Toledo meanwhile suffers the consequences of being deprived of its spiritual leader and chief ecclesiastical authority. Teresa has a personal confrontation with the ecclesiastical governor, Don Gómez Tello de Girón.

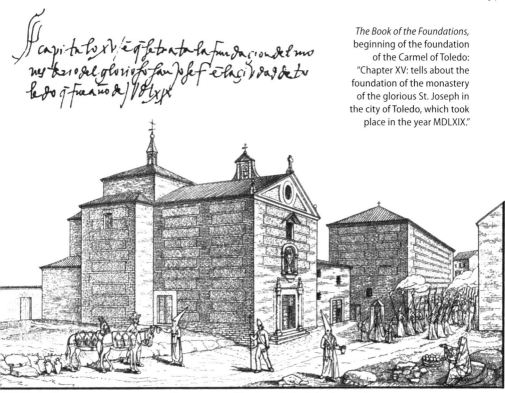

Exterior view of the Carmel of Toledo; drawing by Hye Hoys (1866–1867)

Toledo

ST. JOSEPH'S MONASTERY

MAY 14, 1569

Let's take a walk through Toledo's Jewish quarter. It is mid-May, and in a little while the sun will be quite strong. But right now it is only half light, enough to see the warren of short, narrow, winding streets that seem deliberately designed to hide the famous arabesque-style synagogue.

Panorama of the city of Toledo

Down below, the river Tagus makes one last bend, as if waving farewell on its way to Extremadura. But up here near the synagogue, in a low, cramped little house, Mother Teresa has just inaugurated her fifth monastery of Discalced Carmelite nuns. Let Teresa herself narrate the beginning of the foundation's story: "In the city of Toledo there lived an honorable man, a servant of God, who was a merchant. This man never married. He lived a very devout life, and was very truthful and upright. He conducted his business honestly and amassed wealth only in order to put it to some use that would be pleasing to God. But he became mortally ill. His name was Martín Ramírez" (F 15.1). A Jesuit priest named Pablo Hernández, one of those who accompanied Teresa to Malagón, knew this man and his intentions. He went to see him and suggested that a monastery of Discalced Carmelite nuns would fit the bill admirably. The dying man agreed but left the matter in the hands of his brother, Alonso Álvarez. At which juncture "God took him to Himself."

Cathedral of Toledo, bell tower and façade

When Teresa was in Malagón, then, she knew of this possibility and looked forward to making a foundation in the imperial city of Toledo for a variety of reasons. As we saw, she had a reason for making the Valladolid foundation first but was unable to leave there until near the end of February. From Valladolid she went to Medina, where she decided definitively on the kind of enclosure that her monasteries were to have. From there she visited Duruelo and was amazed to find the once dignified Father Anthony sweeping the porch. According to Teresa's account, "He proclaimed by word and deed that he had swept away the dust of honor and vainglory" (F 14.6). After a short stop at her beloved St. Joseph's, Ávila, to keep in contact with her loved ones there, she was finally on the road for Toledo.

To quote Isabel de Santo Domingo, who was not used to such long trips, they traveled those sixty-six miles "with great propriety, veils down so as not to be seen, and observing our times for mental and vocal prayer." They stayed overnight at Tiemblo and almost experienced the sword of an angry guest whose room they had taken by mistake. Then on through Cadarso de los Vidrios, with its reformed Franciscans so dear to Teresa's heart. After a last stop at San Martín de Valdeiglesias, noted for its fine pines, good wine, and the fortress of the Duke of the Infantado, they reached Toledo on March 24, the vigil of the feast of the Annunciation.

Toledo still retained something of the sparkle of its former splendor. Encircled by three walls, its center still housed enough nobility to cause contemporary chroniclers to refer to it as "the head of the kingdom and the heart of Spain."

The population of the city has been calculated at about 90,000, but they were not as united or as homogeneous as the confining grip of the Tagus might lead us to think. The social stratification, which ranged from showy opulence to the most abject poverty, made its presence felt everywhere, even in monasteries, parishes, and sodalities. These differences, with their accompanying envy and sensitivity on matters of honor, were to have a disturbing effect on the new Carmel too. But for now let's return to the topic at hand.

The three nuns from Ávila entered by the Cambrón Gate and alighted before the welcoming palace of their friend Doña Luisa de la Cerda. With

Door of the Church of San Clemente (Toledo) and view of the choir

Cathedral of Toledo at night

such connections, with the late Martín Ramírez's money a certainty, and with the king's awaited go-ahead only a formality, there was little to worry about. All they really lacked was the archbishop's permission.

A long time ago the Lord said through the mouth of his prophet, "My thoughts are not your thoughts," a sentiment echoed by the proverb "Man proposes, but God disposes." Soon, Teresa would be heard repeating frequently that "God's ways are not our ways."

Teresa immediately set about obtaining ecclesiastical permission. At the time, Archbishop Bartolomé de Carranza was a prisoner of the Inquisition in Valladolid, and nobody (including Doña Luisa) had been able to get anything from the cathedral chapter or from the archbishop's deputy. Their argument was that Toledo already had 1,200 nuns and that they were consequently not allowing any more convents to be founded. That sounds quite reasonable, but it was really only a smokescreen. The real reason had more to do with the bad feelings between the chapter and the administrator, and that the patrons of the proposed foundation did not belong to the nobility. The St. Nicholas district, where they intended to found, was one of the most exclusive in the city and would never tolerate a monastery for poor people, built to honor the memory of a mere merchant.

As if this weren't bad enough, the late Don Martín's merchant relatives also began to be quite uncooperative. So much so, indeed, that Teresa "broke off negotiations with them entirely" (F 15.4).

This second difficulty did not trouble Teresa as much as did the inability to obtain ecclesiastical permission. She decided to take the bull by the horns and confront the administrator himself:

> I decided to speak with the administrator, so I went to a church near his house and sent a messenger to ask if he would see me. We had been two months trying to get his permission and things were going from bad to worse. When we met, I said it was a shame that women who wanted to live a life of austerity and perfection should be hindered from works which were a great service to Our Lord by those who had no desire for such a life and were living a life of ease. This and plenty more I said to him, for the Lord had made me very determined. His heart was moved, and before I left he gave me the permission. (F 15.5)

The vision of the administrator of one of the most powerful sees in Christendom cornered in some obscure sacristy by the forthright logic of an unimportant poor nun says a lot about "God's ways." Nor is that the end of Teresa's surprising tactics. She was delighted that she had the permission at last, but in reality she still had nothing: neither house nor money to rent one. There were no houses to be had in the city, and Don Martín's executors were not parting with a penny.

It was now that Teresa remembered two people who some time previously had promised help. One was Don Alonso de Ávila, a rich merchant; she had not been counting on him for anything because he was very ill at the time. The other was just a "poor student" named Alonso de Andrada. A Franciscan friend of Teresa's had told him to help her if she ever needed anything.

Chalices and patens from the time of St. Teresa

Chest on which the saint wrote *The Interior Castle*

Engraved seal made of steel, used by the saint

As we have indicated, the whole of Toledo had been combed for "a house to rent," and not even the most influential of her friends had been able to find anything. Teresa then suggested to her daughters that they entrust the matter to poor Andrada. They laughed; it wouldn't be right for them even to be seen with him, they said. Teresa paid no attention; she was tired of influence that led nowhere. She felt too that there was some mystery about the tattered student's offer of help; so she asked him if he would find a house. "The following morning when I was at Mass in the Jesuit church he came up and told me that he had found a house. He had the keys, he said, and the house was nearby; would we like to go and view it?" (F 15.7). Imagine the astonishment of the others at this new manifestation of God's ways, an example of his choosing the weak to confound the strong.

With Don Alonso's money the little house was rented, and the nuns moved in immediately with all their "furniture": two mattresses, a blanket, some borrowed articles for saying Mass, and a little handbell. In no time, they had the place just as they wanted it. On May 14, they held the official opening in the by-now-classic Teresian style.

Some time later, Don Martín's famous relatives saw the light and gave enough money to buy a few houses and build a chapel in honor of St. Joseph. At first the community reveled in the numerous visits from the citizens, but they soon saw that this was disturbing their solitude. Because of this they handed over the church to the chaplains and, thirteen years later, when Beatrice of Jesus, Teresa's niece, was prioress, they moved to their present quarters in what had been Doña Luisa de la Cerda's palace.

So Teresa had yet another dovecote. In Spanish the word *quinta* means both "fifth" and "villa." Teresa therefore called this, her fifth foundation, her villa. She liked to go there and rest, and enjoyed better health when she did so.

Toledo meant something special to Teresa, as it did to El Greco. They were both there in 1577 and, although there is no record that the mystic nun and the artist ever met, according to some accounts Teresa influenced

Palace of Doña Luisa de la Cerda

his brilliant creations with suggestions on subject matter and coloring drawn from her own visions.

How full of paradoxes the story of this foundation has been! Let's dwell briefly on just one of them: the immense paradox that the whole infinite mystery of what we call the Church of Christ should be enfleshed in a human and social setup like that of the Church of Toledo, or any other for that matter. Let us look at Teresa's attitude toward the church.

As Teresa witnessed in Toledo, Spain's primatial see, the church was full of human weakness. As noted above, the see was without its archbishop at the time. Ten years previously, Archbishop Carranza had been arrested by the Inquisition, or rather, by a conspiracy of the human frailty of theologians and intellectuals. From prison in Valladolid, he was to go on to prison in Rome, never to be reinstated.

It didn't matter that Carranza had been one of the council fathers at Trent, that he had been King Philip II's advisor, author of a famous catechism, a friend of spiritual people like Luis de Granada, and a truly spiritual man himself. He ran afoul of the powerful theologians of the day—men such as Melchior Cano, Juan de Valdés, and others—and that was enough. Ecclesiastically speaking, Toledo was an orphaned church. The cathedral chapter was not on speaking terms with the administrator, since the latter had tried to take over the see. The whole atmosphere was charged with the ecclesiastical class war we alluded to earlier.

How did Teresa react to this situation? She observed and she took action. Teresa observed, read, listened, and generally kept herself informed of what was going on in Toledo, and indeed everywhere else as well. The conclusion she came to could not have been more dramatic: "The world is burning; they want to crucify Christ again; they want to tear down the church. . . . No, sisters, this is no time to be bothering God with trifling matters!" (WP 1.5).

Teresa took action. She didn't waste time on useless hand-wringing. Nor did she do things just for the sake of doing something. Having taken note of "the great evils in the church," she did not raise her voice to denounce them, nor did she condemn bishops and institutions in the style of St. Bridget of Sweden or St. Catherine of Siena. She began with her own inner conversion. Then she tried to get others to do the same by dotting the map with her Carmels—each of them the church in miniature, where chosen souls fought with the arm of prayer "for the defenders of the church, for the preachers, and for the theologians" (WP 1.3). She would make her nuns the ensigns and standard-bearers in the fight. She would love the church and fight for it. She would submit each and every grace she received from God to its judgment. Her only ideal would be, as she expressed it on her deathbed, "to [be] a daughter of the church."

Proof of Teresa's great respect for "the men of her church" is the litany of ecclesiastical names that fill the pages of her life: Don Álvaro de Mendoza, the first father and patron of her work from its beginnings in Ávila; Francisco de Ribera, that patriarchal figure from Valencia who asked her to come and personally make a foundation there; Don Fernando de Rojas y Sandoval, the bishop who was hostile when she first went to Seville but who later would not let her leave until he had first knelt before her and received her blessing; Diego de León, the Carmelite bishop who acted as intermediary between herself and the Order; the saintly nuncio, Nicolás Ormaneto, who gave his unreserved support to her work; and even St. Pius V, the pope to whom Teresa wrote, though both her letter and his answer have been lost. The list of priests is even longer, many of them the best-known saints and theologians of a period that abounded in both.

And speaking of knowledge and holiness, let us conclude our brief visit to Toledo by pointing out that it was here, on top of that old chest still lovingly preserved by the nuns, that Teresa began the last and most sublime of her works: *The Interior Castle.* We'll say more later of this monument to the human capacity for experiencing God, recounted so powerfully by this foundress and mystic.

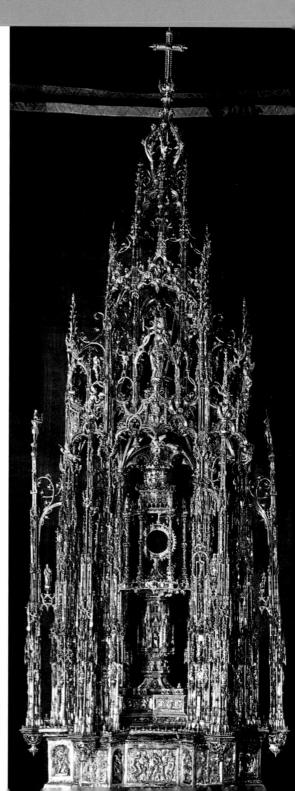

"La Custodia," the 10-foot-tall majestic monstrance of gold, silver and jewels crafted by Enrique de Arfe; cathedral of Toledo

PASTRANA
St. Teresa's Route from Toledo to Pastrana

1569
May

The Princess of Eboli pressures Teresa to found a Carmel at Pastrana.

May 30

Teresa leaves Toledo for Pastrana, with a stop in Madrid.

May 31

The foundress spends eight days as the guest of the Royal Discalced (Franciscan) sisters in Madrid. She meets with two Italian hermits, Maríano Azzaro and Giovanni (Juan) Narduch.

June 23

Foundation of the Pastrana Carmel.

July 10

The Discalced Carmelite friars' monastery is founded at Pastrana. The two Italian hermits take the Carmelite habit and new religious names: Maríano de San Benito and Juan de la Miseria.

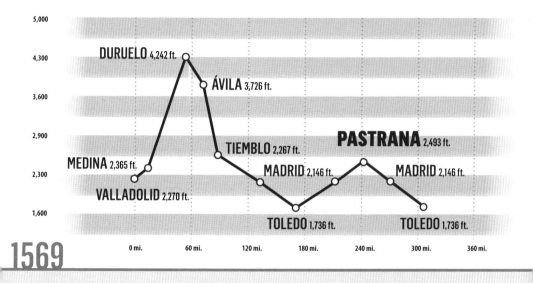

The Book of the Foundations, begins to relate the foundation of the Carmelite monasteries at Pastrana: "Chapter XVII: which treats of the foundations of the monasteries of Pastrana, both for friars and for nuns. This was in the same year MDLXIX."

1569

July 21

Teresa returns to Toledo. She sends Isabel de Santo Domingo to Pastrana as prioress.

A Distressing Episode

The Princess of Eboli, Doña Ana de Mendoza, pesters Teresa to let her read the saint's manuscript, *The Book of Her Life*, and succeeds. Later, after a series of conflicts with Teresa and out of spite, the princess denounces the book to the Inquisition. The inquisitors seize the manuscript and keep it until after Teresa's death. This results in seven years of uncertainty and worry for Teresa, from 1575 to 1582.

Pastrana (Guadalajara)

MONASTERY OF THE CONCEPTION

JUNE 23, 1569

This new foundation might be called "Operation Pastrana" because of several unique factors. Against the backdrop of this mountain village, with its olive groves, fig, and cherry trees, we will meet some individuals who are not normally part of Teresa's scene. Politics plays a part, bringing with it the interplay of important people and the power of money. It also features the simultaneous founding of houses for both friars and nuns. And to crown everything, the whole undertaking ends in partial failure.

Convent of the Conceptionist nuns, former monastery of the Carmelites.
On the previous page, a panorama of Pastrana. Drawings by Hye Hoys (1866–1867)

The story begins in May 1569. Teresa had just put the finishing touches to her Toledo foundation and was enjoying a couple of weeks' peace and quiet. May 29 was Pentecost Sunday and, as Teresa herself tells us,

> that morning when we sat down to eat, I was so relieved at having nothing to do and at the prospect of being able to spend some time with the Lord on this feast that I could hardly eat for happiness. But I must not have deserved such consolation, for while we were eating I was told that a servant of the Princess of Eboli, Ruy Gómez de Silva's wife, was outside. I went out to find that the princess had sent for me. She had been trying for quite a while to have one of our monasteries in Pastrana, but I didn't think it would happen so soon. I was troubled, because the monastery I had just founded was so new and still experiencing some opposition that I didn't think it safe to leave it. So I decided not to go, and told him so. (F 17.2)

The servant was not that easily put off. He had a fine carriage at the door, he said, equipped with everything Teresa would need for the journey. Oh, and by the way . . . the princess was already on her way to Pastrana to meet her! Considering the kind of person the princess was, not to go would be an insult. Teresa was of two minds; how could she please everybody? Ruy Gómez was a very valuable friend, and his wife was not a person to be trifled with. The saint consulted the Lord on the matter and his word was to go; that there was much more than just a foundation involved here. Her confessor confirmed this view, and her mind was made up.

"I left Toledo on [the Monday after Pentecost]. Our journey took us through Madrid, where my companions and I stayed with some Franciscan nuns. The lady who founded that convent was also living with them; she was Doña Leonor de Mascareñas, who had at one time been the king's governess" (F 17.5).

It is worth noting here that up until then, Teresa's reforming enterprise had never had political overtones. Religious reforms were quite fashionable at the time, and there were two clear centers of reformist activity: Rome and Madrid. Rome's vision was ecclesiastical; that of Madrid had a distinctly political slant. Teresa's work was done through the Carmelite prior general in Rome and belonged to the first category. The nearest her work had ever come to involvement with the imperial court was her tiff with the Council of Ávila about the wells near St. Joseph's.

Soon, however, thanks to the Pastrana house, she was to become involved in that small world of powerful people. It is they who now seem to take the initiative in founding; who place the means at her disposal; who get their own interests mixed up in it; and who change Teresa's habitual procedure by substituting plush carriages for muleback or caravan, page boys for muleteers, and dealings with the mighty for the simple but effective Andradas of this world. In this undertaking Teresa would not have to dirty her hands among plasterers and stonemasons. All this, let us add, unwillingly and in obedience to the Voice within.

That said, let us return to her in the convent of the Royal Discalced (Franciscan) nuns she was staying with. Teresa spoke with Doña Leonor, who introduced her to two strange hermits (of whom we'll say more later). Among those who came to visit her was King Philip II's own sister, Doña Juana de Austria, widow of Don Juan of Portugal. Teresa would seem to have made a good impression on the princess, for afterward she was very helpful when Teresa had to deal with the king.

The atmosphere in which Teresa moved during her stay in Madrid is best summed up in the following anecdote about a group of high-ranking ladies who, invited by the Princess of Eboli, came to see the famous nun from

Palace of the Prince and Princess of Eboli

Toledo. To quote a contemporary chronicler: "Many of the leading ladies of Madrid high society came to see her; some out of devotion, others out of curiosity. Some wanted to witness a miracle, others wanted to know the future. Oh, the natural weakness of women! But Teresa's humility was more than equal to such a situation. She spoke simply and plainly to them, and, after the initial polite exchanges were over, she steered the conversation to such neutral subjects as the beauty of the streets of Madrid, and so on."

Teresa spent a week in Madrid. No doubt she also spoke with the Franciscan nuns and influenced them to some degree with her approach and outlook. She certainly made a very favorable impression, as the following passage written by the abbess, Juana de la Cruz, testifies: "Praise God who has permitted us to see a saint whom we can imitate. She eats, sleeps and speaks like the rest of us, and is completely natural and unassuming."

Toward June, just before Corpus Christi, the founding party set off at last for Pastrana: two nuns; the chaplain, Father Pedro Muriel; and Beatriz

Façade and courtyard, convent of the Descalzas Reales (Royal Discalced), Madrid

de Cisneros, a servant of Doña Leonor's who was thinking of becoming a Carmelite nun. In the princess's fast and comfortable coach, the trip was pleasant and short, just two days. They traveled through Alcalá, Villalbilla, Pezuela, and along the Tagus valley to Pastrana. This little town was just then at the height of its glory. Centered on the proud palace of its princely family, it had a population of 827 souls in and around it.

Before going on with the story, let us meet this princely couple, for to understand the story we need to be acquainted with these two individuals. Doña Ana de Mendoza y de la Cerda, the princess, was twenty-nine years old at the time. Some described her as "out of her mind"; others as "a furious and formidable woman." What is certain is that as the only daughter of

The Madrid Gate (Alcalá de Henares)

a very powerful family she was accustomed from childhood to giving free rein to her every whim. Depending on her mood, she could be aggressive, insolent, astute, flattering, generous, or a prude. Perhaps she did have some honesty and piety deep down—but so deep down that they were eclipsed by her other less positive qualities.

On the other hand, her husband, Ruy Gómez, was the soul of discretion and was always struggling to tone down his strident, mercurial wife. Portuguese by birth, he had nevertheless found great favor with the Spanish king. That may be why a contemporary said of him that "After the glory of his God, his only other object in life is the happiness of his king."

Now that we've met our hosts, let's continue. Teresa and her companions were given a truly royal and unforgettable welcome. Still, even now the mother foundress was beginning to feel there was something in the whole atmosphere of the place that would eventually sour their stay here: certain ridiculous demands of the princess, who seemed to regard the nuns as a new toy to play with.

The princess tried to determine exactly how poor the nuns should be, the size of their cells, their daily routine, which novices were suitable, and many other things that Teresa regarded as her own business. Title, money, and favors done or promised gave the princess no right to change the nuns' lifestyle in the slightest.

Heated discussions took place in the palace's ornate drawing room—the princess threatening; Teresa letting it be known she would just go back to Madrid without making any foundation; and the prince, once more, tempering his wife's demands.

Teresa was full of worrying premonitions, but she carried on chiefly because she wanted to see a second house of her Discalced friars there. Finally, after many difficulties, the monastery was officially opened June 23, 1569. With great tact and prudence—and, on Teresa's orders, making a note of every last thing donated by the princess—the sisters managed to survive the next four years. And then Ruy Gómez died. That completely unhinged the princess, and she decided to join the Carmelites! Unlike other applicants, she did not *ask* to be admitted; she *demanded* it. There was no arguing with her about this one-sided decision. She received (or more correctly, gave herself) the habit, but her character remained the same. Although the youngest by rank in the monastery, she tried to have her way in everything. Finally, she was expelled. The furious, sulking princess returned to her palace determined to get revenge. She had tricked Teresa into letting her have a copy of her *Life,* and she now ridiculed it both in private and in public. But that wasn't the end of her vengeance. She denounced Teresa's book to the Inquisition, took back everything she had given the nuns, broke the endowment contract, and subjected them to whatever humiliation she could think of. To put an end to so sorry a state of affairs, Teresa told her nuns to leave Pastrana a year later. She took them to Segovia instead.

Descent to the hermits' caves

As we've mentioned, the fact that Teresa was trying to make a male foundation as well as a female one was always a complicating factor in the Pastrana undertaking. She had permission from the prior general for two such foundations. One was already established in Duruelo; she had planned the other for Pastrana.

This is where the two men she was introduced to in Madrid by Doña Leonor come in. Both were Italians; one was Maríano Azzaro, the other Giovanni Narduch. According to Teresa, the former was "a doctor and very ingenious"; the latter more imaginative and artistic. Both were half pilgrim and half hermit. Ever in search of a place of austere solitude, with the help of Doña Leonor and Ruy Gómez, they eventually ended up in Pastrana. There Gómez gave them a hermitage to fulfill their cherished dreams.

For Teresa, to meet two hermits who had a hermitage in Pastrana was an obvious act of Providence. Here is how she described her interview with Maríano:

> When he described his way of life to me, I showed him a copy of our primitive Rule and told him he would have little trouble observing all of it; it was the same as his way of life, especially where manual work was concerned. . . . When I explained how much he could serve the Lord in our habit, he said he would think about it that night. . . . His Majesty loved him, and so moved him that on the following day he called me and told me his mind was made up. The speed with which he changed his mind surprised him, especially since it was a woman who changed it for him. (F 17.9)

When Maríano changed his mind, so did Giovanni. Before leaving Pastrana, therefore, Teresa obtained the provincial's permission to convert the hermitage into a friary; Maríano and Giovanni and a Father Baltasar de Jesús formed the little community, officially founded on July 13. Maríano took San Benito as his religious title; Giovanni became Juan de la Miseria, the name with which he was later to sign his famous portrait of Mother Teresa.

Stated so briefly, all this sounds a lot simpler and more straightforward than it was in reality. This second friars' foundation was to cause Teresa more than her share of heartaches. Removed from their favorite state of being solitary hermits, the trio was also encouraged by penitential extremes then in vogue—including the extravagances of a certain Catalina de Cardona, of whom we'll say more in a moment. Combined with the lack of wisdom and prudence associated with the kind of holiness John of the Cross had established at Duruelo, the new recruits soon slipped into an excessive form of penance that had a strong influence on the newly founded Discalced Carmelite friars.

Nevertheless, there were Discalced Carmelite friars in Pastrana until the expulsion of the religious orders in 1835. Today their house, with major structural changes, is home to a community of Franciscan friars.

On the following page:
St. Teresa gives the Rule of the reform
to Fray Maríano

V. PE AMBROSIO M.ª RIANO ITALIANO DYLVS RELINGE DOC.ª EN AMB.ºD
RECHO EL OCVENT.ᵐᵒˢ IDGR.ꜰˢ VIRTVDES ASISTIO A. S.ᵗᵒ CON.ᵗⁱᵒᵈ REN
TOR A JOLE A. ORD.N N.R A S.ᵐ ERESA PAR.A FVND.Æ EL COMB.ᵗᵒᵈ PAST.ᵃ
LE EN GRAND CE POR LO MVCHO Q.ᵉ RABAJO EN EL DSCA CEZ FV
PRIMERE RECTOR DLA PROBINCIA DPOR.TVG.A. M.ᵗⁱᵒ EN M.ᶜ CONA
SISENCIA DL OSM.ᴮ S S.ᴺ COME IS. DAMIAN EL AÑO D 1594

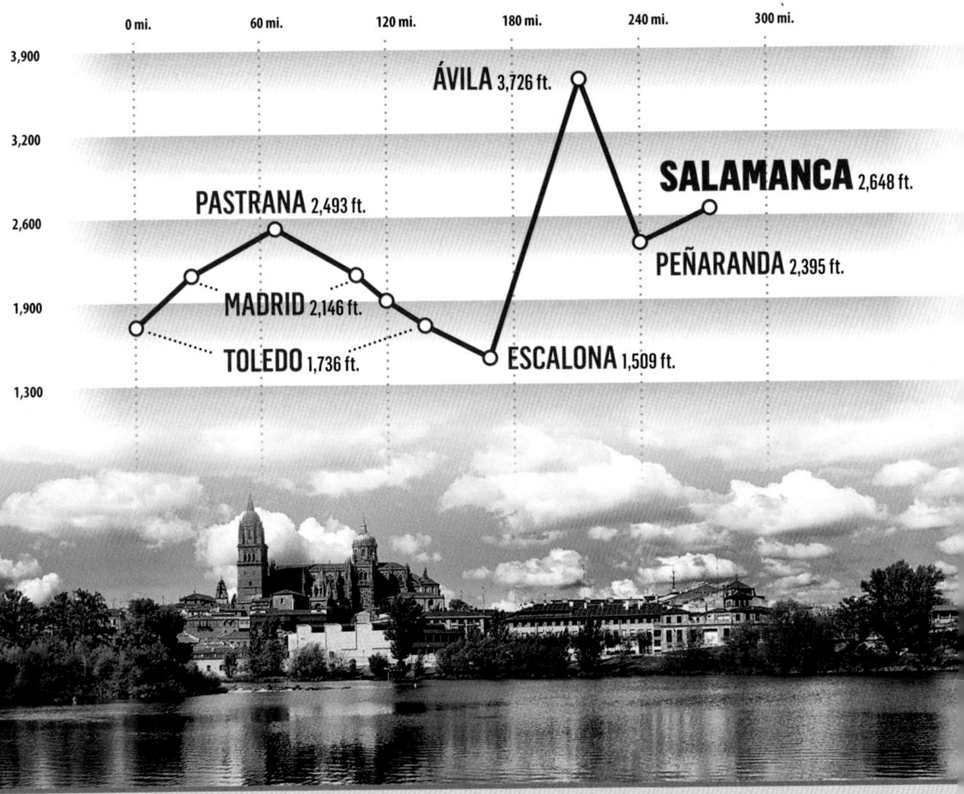

Chart of St. Teresa's travels in 1570
the Salamanca foundation

The chart shows elevation along St. Teresa's route with markers:
- PASTRANA 2,493 ft.
- MADRID 2,146 ft.
- TOLEDO 1,736 ft.
- ÁVILA 3,726 ft.
- ESCALONA 1,509 ft.
- SALAMANCA 2,648 ft.
- PEÑARANDA 2,395 ft.

Horizontal axis: 0 mi., 60 mi., 120 mi., 180 mi., 240 mi., 300 mi.
Vertical axis: 1,300, 1,900, 2,600, 3,200, 3,900

SALAMANCA
St. Teresa's Route from Toledo to Salamanca

1570
May

The Toledo community relocates to the Ramirez house.

July 10

Teresa returns to Pastrana; there she attends the profession of Maríano de San Benito and Juan de la Miseria.

Mid-August

Teresa sets out from Toledo for Ávila and Salamanca.

October 31

She arrives in Salamanca.

November 1

Foundation of the Carmel of Salamanca. The two nuns spend the famous "night at the students' house." On the same day the Carmelite friars establish their college, or house of studies, at Alcalá de Henares.

The Book of the Foundations, begins to relate the foundation of the Carmel of Salamanca: "Chapter XVIII: treats of the foundation of the monastery of St. Joseph [Josef rather than Jose in original)] in Salamanca, which was in the year MDLXX. Deals with some important advice for the prioresses . . ."

1570

The Pace Quickens

Salamanca and Alcalá are the most important university cities of the time—seats of learning and a crossroads for Spanish youth. For her part, Mother Teresa is "in favor of learning." For her, "learning" means biblical and humanistic culture. She is a great admirer of scholars: "I have never been deceived by a learned man," she writes.

At the same time she is founding the Carmel in Salamanca, she establishes a house of studies for her young friars in Alcalá. Soon after, she sends Fray John of the Cross there as rector. She also works tirelessly to set up another house of studies in Salamanca. (She will succeed toward the end of her life, in 1581.) Both colleges will attain fame for their celebrated "Salamanca Courses" (in theology) and "Alcalá Course" (in philosophy).

Salamanca

Exterior view
of the Carmel
of Salamanca;
drawing by
Hye Hoys
(1866–1867)

ST. JOSEPH'S MONASTERY

NOVEMBER 1, 1570

In his popular *Life of St. Teresa*, the late Father Crisógono de Jesús, one of the finest modern writers of spiritual literature in Spanish, summed up the story of one of Teresa's costliest foundations in this fine passage:

> Four months have passed, and it is All Souls' Night 1570 in Salamanca. The city is subdued as a hundred bells ring out from churches and monasteries, sounding like one long groan from souls floating restlessly above their belfries and towers.
>
> In an empty mansion to the north of the city two nuns are busy barring ill-fitting doors and windows. They

are Mother Teresa and Sister María del Sacramento, just arrived from Ávila after a cold, wet journey. They have come to make a foundation. A few moments earlier the old mansion was shaking from the racket caused by the students who were refusing to hand it over to the nuns. Now the great old building, with its large rooms, wide passages, and endless attics, was silent once more. The funeral toll of the city bells and the howling wind came through the crevices in the windows, sighing and moaning.

Teresa's companion is afraid: afraid of the students, some of whom could still be hiding in any nook or cranny; afraid of the dead, groaning among the towers. Teresa laughs at her frightened sister, who keeps looking over her shoulder as if she expects the shadows to creep up on her, or ghosts to come in through the closed doors.

At last, the long, hard day took its toll and they settled down on some straw to sleep, covered with a few old borrowed blankets. Sister María was still restless. She thought of the dead and looked round every time a board creaked.

"What are you looking at?" asked Teresa. "Can't you see that nobody can come in?"

"Mother," she replied, "I was thinking, what would you do here alone if I were to die now?"

"Sister, if that happens I'll think of something. Right now, just let me get some sleep."

Minutes later, the two nuns were sound asleep on their bed of straw, snug in their borrowed blankets.

At dawn, all fears and shadows gone, they are up and assembling a modest wooden altar. They tidy up hallways, rooms, and stairs, left in a mess by the students. The first Mass is celebrated, and the foundation is established. Mother Teresa is happy in her rambling, old mansion and pokes fun at Sister María about her fears of the night before.

The Salamanca undertaking, however, was not as funny as that; nor did it take place so quickly.

From Pastrana, Teresa had gone to Toledo, a place she always found stimulating. There she either began or wrote her greatest works. Then on to

Ávila, because the bishop was becoming a little alarmed at the length of her absence from a community of which she was prioress.

"While I was attending to this, the Jesuit rector at Salamanca wrote to me, giving me reasons why it would be good to have one of our monasteries in that city" (F 18.1). Teresa wasn't sure. But she trusted in her unfailing God rather than in the reasons given her. She trusted, too, in her hardworking and poverty-loving nuns who needed little to live on. And she trusted in the help of loyal friends like the merchant Nicolás Gutiérrez (father of many nuns, including some Carmelites). Armed with that confidence, Teresa decided to embark on yet another foundation.

The more experienced she became in this business of foundations, the more cautious Teresa became. This time she asked for permission of the bishop of Salamanca before leaving Ávila. The Jesuit rector, who had achieved a certain amount of fame as a chronicler of the Council of Trent, obtained this for her immediately. Another precaution she took was to not bring her nuns with her, thus avoiding the risk of not having a place for them to live, as happened at Medina. This time she went with just one companion, to make sure that the house rented by Father Julian of Ávila was in order.

Accompanied by two Carmelite Fathers of the Observance, Teresa set out for Salamanca. Some sixty miles and several stops later, they reached their destination. "We arrived on the vigil of All Saints, having traveled much of the way by night and in bitter cold. . . . I was not at all well" (F 18.3).

She must have been quite sick, because it was only when writing of this foundation that she alluded to the physical hardships of her founding expeditions: "When describing these foundations I don't say anything of the hardships endured along the way: the cold, the heat and the snow. At times it snowed all day, sometimes we got lost, other times I was so ill and feverish. Praise God, my health is usually poor, but I've always been conscious that God was giving me strength" (F 18.4).

It was here in Salamanca, by order of Father Jerónimo Ripalda, that Teresa began writing *The Book of the Foundations*, a book she would go on writing up until a few days of her death. Here, with the simplicity of genius, she tells the story of her reforming work, the bad times as well as the good,

Bridge over the Tormes River with the cathedral of Salamanca in the background

Courtyard of the "House of St. Teresa"

The University of Salamanca

from the first to the last foundation. Its pages are a hymn of praise to God, praise expressed through events in which he took part. They need to be read in the same spirit of praise in which they were written. A copy in Teresa's own hand is in the Escorial Library.

Salamanca's claim to fame rests on its university. Its 7,000 students provided the nation with an unending flow of cardinals, bishops, council fathers, viceroys, inquisitors, royal counselors, and all the other intellectuals of the social and political elite that ruled half the world and enhanced the name of the city.

That is the good side. Salamanca's university halls were also the sounding board for a thousand and one problems from all over the realm, as well as from Rome and the Americas. The tensions of the day left their mark on the cloisters, and the academic climate was highly polemical.

To give just one example, in 1561 the Augustinian friar Luis de León translated the Song of Songs from the original Hebrew. In 1570 he was expounding on the Latin translation (known as the Vulgate) in opposition to León de Castro, an enemy of the Hebrew specialists. The hall he lectured in still stands. In 1571 Bartolomé de Medina—a close friend of St. Teresa's—drew up a list of seventeen statements attributed to Fray Luis, resulting in the latter's imprisonment by the Inquisition from March 1572

The "Ecce Homo," a painting bought by St. Teresa for the Salamanca foundation; *at right,* the saint's finger and another relic

to March 1576. When he was released from prison, Fray Luis returned to the lecture hall and took to the teaching podium with the celebrated phrase: "As we were saying yesterday . . ."

It was, then, a lively student world. And Teresa arrived in the middle of it just about the time students returned for the new academic year. It was not the easiest time to find a house to rent. She solved this problem, as we've seen; and with the little money she had with her, she bought two important items of furniture for the new foundation: a painting of the *Ecce Homo* and a painting of Our Lady receiving Christ from the Cross.

They were not in their old mansion long before it became obvious that it had certain drawbacks. The building itself was not very sound, but its location was an even greater handicap—its proximity to the river Tormes and the city reservoir made life intolerable. Soon, the health of the nuns was affected, and the house was declared unfit to house the Blessed Sacrament. This was the last straw; it was time to consider moving.

We have to pause here, however, and allow Teresa to attend to other business before she can focus on the move. Business took her to Alba; some very unpleasant difficulties demanded her presence in the Medina and Ávila houses for a time; and she was also called on to make peace in her old monastery of the Incarnation. Then she set out again for Salamanca.

After a rather eventful trip—one time the mule carrying their money got lost, and another time the whole group did!—Teresa reached Salamanca on July 13, 1571. The party first visited the house that they intended to buy. It was located between Plaza de San Benito and Calle de los Doctrinos, the latter now named after the Jesuits. It was owned by a certain Pedro de la Vanda, but legal formalities were holding up proceedings. Teresa was in a hurry, since the new tenants of the former property were putting pressure on the nuns to move out. Fortunately, the owner allowed Teresa to go ahead with the rather substantial remodeling that was needed. Getting this house ready was going to take a long time . . .

The little community spent all they had (that is, all the individual nuns' dowries) turning this building into a monastery, complete with cloister, cells, refectory, and chapel. Teresa found the money to buy an ornate "reredos depicting Our Lady, with St. Joseph on one side and St. Bartholomew on the other, and including both God the Father and St. Mary Magdalen as well."

With this heavenly court installed, all was ready for the monastery's formal founding. This time it was quite a solemn one, Teresa tells us: "There was a large congregation present and we had music; the Blessed Sacrament was installed with great solemnity" (F 19.10). The preacher for the occasion was the city's most acclaimed, Diego de Estella.

But Teresa's troubles were far from over. "The very next day—to temper our joy at having the Blessed Sacrament—the owner of the house came. He was so angry I didn't know what to do with him; and it must have been the devil who made sure he couldn't see reason, for we had fulfilled all the conditions in the contract. I decided to give him the house back, but he didn't want that either" (F 19.10). What Pedro de la Vanda—or rather his wife, who put him up to it—really wanted was money "to settle two daughters." The contract had not required payment of this money until the king's solution to the legal technicalities was obtained.

Writing three years later, St. Teresa remarked that the purchase had not yet been finalized. In fact it took forty-four years, during which they were evicted twice, before the nuns were finally settled in that house. They left it

The magnificent Renaissance façade of the Dominican Church of San Esteban (St. Stephen)

only in 1970, when they moved to Cabrerizos, adjacent to the city. No wonder Teresa wrote, "In no monastery of this first Rule have the nuns suffered anything like the trials they had in this one" (F 19.12).

But happily it was also in Salamanca that the Lord granted Teresa very clear proof of his help and many mystical graces. A chief instrument of God's help was the Jesuit, Father Martín Gutiérrez. It was he who had invited Teresa to Salamanca. He and his fellow Jesuits welcomed her and used all their influence in her favor. Above all, she was able to talk openly to him about everything, and sometimes spent whole evenings with him just talking about God. Soon, however, Father Gutíerrez was taken prisoner by French Huguenots and died in captivity. His loss left Teresa bereft: "God help me," she wrote, "I wish I wasn't so fond of God's servants; then I wouldn't miss them so much."

Teresa's mystical graces were so frequent during this time that it was hard to hide their external effects. According to the testimony of Isabel de Jesus, "When she heard me sing a little couplet expressing a longing for God, she was so enraptured that after a time she had to be carried back to her cell in a state of apparent unconsciousness." The couplet in question was:

Confessional used by St. Teresa in the Church of San Esteban, Salamanca

Let my eyes see You,
Kind Sweet Jesus,
Let my eyes see You,
And then let me die.

This then is the story of how the Teresian seed took root in the hard soil of this land of learning, the great Salamanca. One of the characteristic features of Teresian spirituality, in fact, is respect for learning. It is worth reflecting on this for a moment, since we happen to be speaking of the mother foundress's presence in a seat of learning. Many influences went into the formation of Teresa's teachings. The most important and the most obvious influence is that of God himself. But the teachings of many learned men of the day certainly had a strong influence on her too.

Teresa was in touch with the best theologians and consulted the best-qualified confessors. She also knew people famous for their holiness, men like Juan de Ávila and Fray Luis de León, and was on intimate terms with souls as wholly spiritual as John of the Cross. All these encounters found a ready response in her fertile mind and heart. Even if not to the same extent, all these learned and holy men enriched Teresa's life and spirit, and for this she was eternally grateful to all of them.

Well aware of the limitations placed on women in the church and society of her day, Teresa looked to them all for teaching, discernment, security, and support—and not just for herself but also for her daughters and anyone else who wanted to follow her counsels. "I have never been deceived by a learned man," she wrote.

Father Domingo Báñez, one of her favorite confessors, once remarked, "She preferred learned men to those who were merely devout."

Fierce controversy raged in her day between theologians and "spirituals." She was undoubtedly one of the latter, among whom she had many close friends. But she sided with the theologians. They, she thought, have the Bible, theology, and philosophy—what she understood by "learning"— and these things were light for the searching soul. Still, she did not want the theologian to speak from hearsay; she wanted him grounded in experience.

Teresa took the best of both worlds; she teaches on the basis of both. She is brimming with experience yet hungry for the light that books and theologians can cast on it. That is how she came to be a Doctor of the Church.

In the last years of her life, she was thrilled to see the Discalced Carmelite friars also making a foundation in Salamanca and sending their students to the university. In her last letter to Father Jerome Gracián, she told him that students should not be overburdened with either tasks or penances that would interfere with their studies.

Detail of the bronze monument to Fray Luis de León located in front of the University of Salamanca

ALBA de TORMES
St. Teresa's Route to Salamanca – Alba – Ávila

1569
October 26

Pope Pius V names the Dominican Pedro Fernández as visitator of the Carmelites in Castile.

1570
December 3

The deeds are signed for the foundation of the convent at Alba.

1571
January 25

The Carmel of Alba is founded. St. John of the Cross attends the dedication.

Early February

Teresa returns to Salamanca.

April

Teresa travels to Medina, and from there to Ávila.

April 6

Father Juan Bautista Rubeo gives Mother Teresa new permits to enable her to continue making new foundations.

April 15 (Easter)

At recreation, Sister Isabel, a novice, sings a song, "Would That My Eyes Could See You," which sends St. Teresa into ecstasy.

July 10

Appointed by the visitator, Teresa accepts the post of prioress of the Incarnation, Ávila.

August–September

Teresa again is at the Carmel of Medina.

Early October

Teresa leaves Medina and returns to Ávila. On October 6 she begins her three-year term as prioress at the Incarnation.

1572
March 25

Jerome Gracián makes his profession at Pastrana. He will later be provincial of the Teresian reform and one of Teresa's closest collaborators.

Historical Background

Religious persecution in England; Queen Elizabeth I is excommunicated (1570).

The Battle of Lepanto (October 7, 1571): the

Holy League defeats the main fleet of the Ottoman Empire off the coast of Greece, saving the region from Muslim domination.

The "St. Bartholomew's Night Massacre" (August 23–24, 1572) in Paris. Assassinations and mob violence were directed against French Huguenots (Calvinists) by Catholics protesting a royal marriage that would put a Protestant on the throne of France. Considered by historians as the worst of the century's religious massacres, it resulted in as many as 30,000 deaths.

Pope St. Pius V and St. Francis Borgia die in Rome (1572).

The trial of the Augustinian theologian Luis de León by the Inquisition begins in Salamanca (1572).

Begins to describe the foundation of the Carmel of Alba in *The Book of the Foundations:* "Chapter XX: which treats of the foundation of the monastery of Our Lady of the Annunciation which is in Alba de Tormes. This was in the year MDLXXI."

Graph of St. Teresa's travels in 1571
the Alba foundation

1571

Exterior view of the Carmel of Alba; drawing by Hye Hoys (1866–1867)

Alba de Tormes

MONASTERY OF OUR LADY OF THE ANNUNCIATION

JANUARY 25, 1571

Like Salamanca, Alba is on the right bank of the river Tormes—hence the town's "surname," so to speak. But Alba is located upstream. Only a small plateau, crossed by an ancient Roman paved highway, separates them. Two little hamlets punctuate the sixteen-mile journey, and then the slow descent begins through gently undulating countryside to the Tormes, dominating the fertile plain below, a plain that stretches to the Sierra de Gredos on the horizon. Just before the final descent the view is magnificent.

To the right is the Hieronymite (Religious of St. Jerome) monastery of St. Leonard with its Gothic church and splendid colonnade. Beyond, the belfries and steeples of parish and convent churches rise above the houses. And on a high ridge the proud castle of the dukes of Alba with its six gilded towers is beautifully framed against the bright blue sky of Castile. The medieval bridge, with its twenty-six arches spanning the Tormes, completes the picture.

In Teresa's day the Duke of Alba was one of the most important men in the realm. So great was his influence with Philip II that even men like the Prince of Eboli could reach the king only through him.

However, he had nothing to do with Teresa's coming to Alba. Neither did she come because she liked the idea of making a foundation there. "I was not very enthusiastic about it, because since it was a small town the community would need an endowment, and I preferred not to have any" (F 20.1).

The request came from a couple in Salamanca—Don Francisco Velázquez, treasurer of the University of Salamanca, and his wife, Doña Teresa de Layz, who was a native of Alba. Teresa's sister Juana and brother-in-law Juan de Ovalle had a hand in it too; they were friends of the couple and lived nearby.

Teresa goes into great detail about how this couple came to want a monastery of Discalced Carmelite nuns. Let's hear the story from her. Teresa Layz was born into a Castilian family, but she was not exactly welcomed. "Her parents already had four children, all girls. When they saw that the fifth, Teresa Layz, was yet another daughter they were very upset" (F 20.2). As a result of this disappointment and human neglect, the baby received very little attention in the first days of her life.

> Things got so bad that, as if they didn't care whether the child lived or not, they left her alone all day when she was only three days old. They had at least done one good thing for the baby; they had her baptized when she was born. That evening a woman who was concerned and knew what was going on, ran to see if the baby was dead. Others who

Castle of the Dukes of Alba

had come to visit the mother followed her and were witnesses to what I am now about to relate.

The woman took the crying baby in her arms and said: "Now, now, little one, aren't you a Christian?" referring to the cruelty with which she had been treated. The baby raised her head and said: "Yes, I am." She didn't speak again until the normal age at which children start talking. Those who heard her were astonished, and from then on her mother began to love and cherish her. She often said afterwards that she wanted to live long enough to see what God had in store for this child.

The first thing God did was to provide her with a husband who, as well as being virtuous and rich, doted on his wife. "He sought to please her in everything. And well he might, for the Lord gave her everything a husband could ask for in a wife" (F 20.5). That husband was Don Francisco Velázquez.

The only thing that God apparently had not given this exemplary couple was children. The couple wanted children very much and prayed for them. Doña Teresa prayed especially to St. Andrew with this intention. Time passed, until one day "the lady, still as anxious as ever to have a family, seemed to see herself in a house which had a well in the courtyard beneath

Basilica of St. Teresa in Alba; under construction

the gallery. She also saw a green meadow with white flowers all through it, beautiful beyond description. St. Andrew appeared beside the well, as a venerable and handsome old man. . . . 'The children you will have are different to those you desire,' he said. . . . She understood clearly . . . that it was God's will that she should found a monastery" (F 20.7).

Providence, without our knowing, weaves the fabric of our lives. And into this fabric God now wove another thread: the Duchess of Alba decided that she would like the university treasurer to look after the financial management of her estates. One did not refuse the duchess, and so it was that Don Francisco moved from Salamanca to Alba, for less interesting work and a poorer house.

But what was Doña Teresa's surprise when on taking possession of the house she found it was the house she had seen in her vision, complete with courtyard and well! This so moved her that "she decided to turn it into a monastery." All that remained now was to choose her "adopted family" from among the great variety of religious orders. Someone told her that nuns should be ruled out as "most of them were unhappy people." A Franciscan friar, however, suggested that Mother Teresa's nuns seemed to fit Doña Teresa's description of what she was looking for. "Between ourselves and the

Hieronymites," he said, "this place has enough friars." The fact that Doña Teresa was looking for a small, austere, strictly enclosed community certainly pointed in the direction of the Carmelites. The fact that their famous foundress was only down the road in Salamanca and that her sister was a friend of the founding couple clinched the matter.

"At last agreement was reached and an adequate endowment arranged. What impressed me most was that they left their own house to us and moved to a humbler one themselves. The Blessed Sacrament was reserved and the foundation made on the Feast of St. Paul's Conversion 1571" (F 20.14). Teresa had now reached the halfway stage of her foundations; she was fifty-six.

At the beginning of chapter 20 in her *Book of the Foundations*, devoted to the Alba foundation, Teresa complained of one thing: the attitude of people who, ignorant of God's purpose, behave like Doña Teresa's parents in their resentment at having daughters rather than sons. They do so because they fail to realize the great benefits that having daughters can bring or the great harm that having sons can bring; they are unwilling to leave everything to the One who understands everything. "How many fathers will go to hell for having had sons, and how many mothers will go to heaven on account of the daughters they had!" (F 20.3).

This little outburst from Teresa provides us with an opportunity to say something about her feminism. Today, rightly, people are very sensitive about neglected sectors of society. Consequently, strong movements are emerging on behalf of the rights of minorities. Teresa was very conscious of the fact that in her day, women were in this category. They were discriminated against because of their gender. Worse, there was nothing they could do about it. So, in chapter 3 of the *Way of Perfection*, Teresa launched a spirited defense of women, appealing even to the judgment of Christ himself. The censor deleted this from the first edition, but now it is restored and we can read the truly prophetic passage for ourselves:

> When you walked on this earth, Lord, You did not despise women; rather,
> You always helped them and showed great compassion towards them. And

Entrance to the Church of the Annunciation, next to the monastery

You found as much love and more faith in them than You did in men. Among them was your most Blessed Mother, and through her merits we merit what, because of our offenses, we do not deserve. Is it not enough, Lord, that the world has intimidated us . . . so that we may not do anything worthwhile for You in public or dare to speak some truths that we lament over in secret, without Your also failing to hear so just a petition? I do not believe, Lord, that this could be true of Your goodness and justice, for You are a just judge and not like those of the world. Since the world's judges are sons of Adam and all of them men, there is no virtue in women that they do not hold suspect. (WP 3.9)

In her conviction that women were as valuable in God's eyes as men are, Teresa found an ally in a man of proven holiness, St. Peter of Alcántara. In fact, speaking to Teresa, he went even further than she had: "God grants His favors to many more women than men," he stated. He added that women made far greater progress in the way of prayer, and he gave many reasons in favor of women (see L 40.8).

Day after day Teresa saw for herself how God showered his favors on her dovecotes just as soon as they filled up. How, then, was one to explain why men kept women in the wings of the socio-religious stage when God himself seemed determined to give them leading roles?

Teresa was fully aware of her own unimportance. She even seemed to have a bit of a complex about it, always saying she was frail and ignorant. But she loved learning, as we've seen, and highly esteemed learned men. She would stand for no second-class citizenship in the world of knowledge; she and her daughters would be trained, educated in what concerned their way of life. She learned from theologians and confessors and, in turn, taught her sisters, orally and through the written word. As time went on, she attached increasing importance to this kind of education.

The foundress spelled out clearly the role her nuns were to play in society and in the church. She thought big: the universal church was to be the object of their prayers, thoughts, and mortifications.

If we look at the dominant theme of today's feminism—that women have "come of age" and are on an equal footing with their traditional male counterparts and teachers, that they are equals in will and courage—we find it abundantly foreshadowed in Teresa's thinking. Teresa's fearlessness is proverbial, even legendary. Normally she shunned self-praise, but where courage was concerned she admitted, "They say I have no little courage, and it has been seen that God has given me more than is usual in a woman" (L 8.7).

She lived in vigorous times, times charged with the exploits of conquistadors who conquered new worlds for their king. But it was always men who did these things. And the word "man" came to conjure up a picture of courage, effort, daring, and capacity for sacrifice. Teresa fought against the monopolizing of these "manly" qualities by men; they were *human* qualities, and just as much within the reach of women as of men. "The Lord will make them so manly that they will astonish men," she said of her nuns (WP 7.8).

Teresa's life is full of examples of her *muy determinada determinación*— her "very determined determination." From the time when, as a child, she convinced her brother to go off with her to be beheaded by the Moors for Christ to the time when, as an adult, she committed her life fully to Christ, Teresa's life is full of examples of her characteristic determination.

Whenever she was faced with a problem, her attitude was always the same: "It is very important to be quite determined not to stop till you reach the end of the road, no matter what happens, what it costs, or what anybody says . . . even if you die in the attempt . . . or if the world itself should come to an end" (WP 21.1).

All her courage and daring had a solid foundation, however. That foundation was the love of her God. All that mattered to Teresa was to know that whatever she undertook was God's will. To find this out she prayed and sought advice; but once she knew, "forward" was her only gear.

When people sympathized with her in her difficulties, when people saw her poor health and urged her to rest and leave aside this troublesome

Interior of the church and detail of St. Teresa's tomb, Carmel of Alba de Tormes

business of founding monasteries, she would smile and say, "That wouldn't be loving God, would it?"

That, then, is Teresa's style of feminism. Love of being a woman, a love born of her admiration for her mother, Doña Beatriz, and developed by her devotion to Mary, blessed among women.

Her greatest reward in this area was that marvelous and select group of women who gathered around her "to do what little they could" to solve the evils that beset the church.

Some of the women who helped her deserve to be called cofoundresses of her monasteries: Doña Guiomar de Ulloa in Ávila; Doña Luisa de la Cerda in Malagón; Doña María de Mendoza in Valladolid; Doña Teresa de Layz in Alba; Doña Catalina de Tolosa in Burgos. There were others who went a step further and became nuns themselves: Doña Ana Jimena in Segovia and Doña Catalina de Sandoval in Beas.

She had a train of admirers: Queen Juana of Portugal; nobility such as Doña Leonor de Mascareñas; famous penitents like Catalina de Cardona; simple housewives like Juana Dantisco, Father Gracián's mother; and humble village folk too numerous to mention.

The names of certain children have also become associated with Teresa's memory: there was her niece, Teresita, Lorenzo's daughter and later a nun under Teresa's guidance in the Seville Carmel; Father Gracián's sister, Isabel, in the Toledo Carmel; and Antonio Gaytán's daughter, who was admitted to the Alba monastery at the tender age of seven. Teresa lavished affection on all of these, seeing in them future strong women who would, no doubt, put the fear of God into the strong men of Castile.

Singling out the more prominent of Teresa's early Carmelite sisters is far more challenging. Yet there are a few who must be mentioned: María de San José Salazar, the prioress of Seville, is one; she has left us an accurate portrait of the saint in her writings and perhaps reproduced it even more accurately in her own life. Anne of Jesus Lobera was so outstanding that St. John of the Cross dedicated his *Spiritual Canticle* to her, as did Fray Luis de León his edition of *St. Teresa's works*. María Bautista de Ocampo was that enthusiastic niece who first suggested the idea of the reform to

Church of St. John of the Cross

her aunt Teresa. Anne of St. Bartholomew, her nurse and secretary, later brought Discalced Carmel to France, the Netherlands and today's Belgium (together with Anne of Jesus) and is today among those honored by the church as Blessed. María de Jesús, whom Teresa teasingly called her "little scholar," has also been beatified. These and many more constitute her crown and glory both as a saint and as a woman.

But as Teresa herself would say, we digress. It is a worthwhile digression, however. Nor have we finished with Alba: how Teresa came to die here; the description of her famous relics; and a few other matters deserve separate treatment. They will constitute the last chapter of this story.

SEGOVIA Teresa's Itinerary: 1571–1574

1572
Spring

Teresa sends John of the Cross as confessor for the nuns at the Incarnation in Ávila.

1573
February

Teresa travels to Alba and Salamanca.

August 25

In Salamanca, Mother Teresa begins writing *The Book of the Foundations.*

September 28

The Salamanca community moves to Pedro de la Vandá's houses.

1574
March

Teresa and John of the Cross leave Alba for Segovia; they arrive March 10.

March 19

Foundation of the Segovia Carmel.

April 6–7

The nuns from Pastrana arrive at Segovia, having left the Pastrana monastery in the hands of the infamous Princess of Eboli.

September 30

Teresa again sets out from Segovia for Ávila.

October 6

She ends her term as prioress of the Incarnation, Ávila.

Late December

Teresa goes to Valladolid to settle a dispute between Casilda de Padilla and her family.

A Woman's Leadership

Mother Teresa unexpectedly found herself in charge of a diverse group and responsible for a vast spiritual movement. Without claiming the juridical or formal command for herself, she was in fact mother, teacher, leader, and the living embodiment of the group's ideals. She knew how to surround herself with good people and promoted them to positions of responsibility. She traveled because she wanted to be present right in the midst of the most difficult situations that arose. Through her correspondence, she kept up an open dialogue with all concerned, one based on friendship, teaching, and leadership.

The foundation of the Carmel of Segovia as told in *The Book of the Foundations:* Chapter XXI: treats of the foundation of the glorious St. Joseph of the Carmel of Segovia. It was founded on the same day as the feast of St. Joseph, year MDLXXIIII."

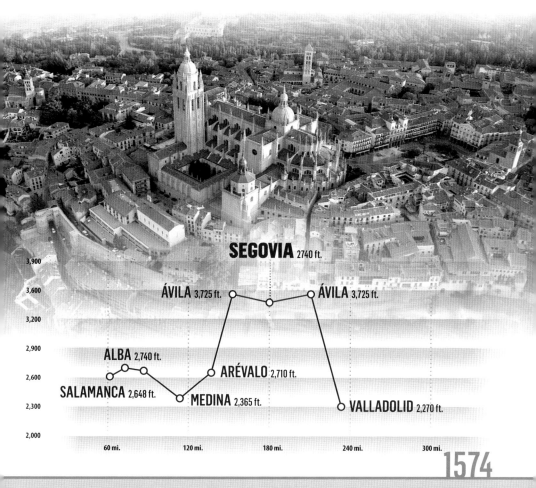

SEGOVIA 2740 ft.

ÁVILA 3,725 ft.   ÁVILA 3,725 ft.

ALBA 2,740 ft.

ARÉVALO 2,710 ft.

SALAMANCA 2,648 ft.

MEDINA 2,365 ft.   VALLADOLID 2,270 ft.

3,900
3,600
3,200
2,900
2,600
2,300
2,000

60 mi.   120 mi.   180 mi.   240 mi.   300 mi.

1574

Chart of the trip to Segovia and from Segovia to Valladolid

Segovia

MONASTERY OF ST. JOSEPH OF CARMEL

MARCH 19, 1574

Just as Castile had grown at the speed of El Cid's horse, so now Carmel was growing at the pace of Teresa's covered wagon. But there were some who looked on its progress as if it were a kind of oil spill oozing uncontained across the broad plains of Castile. For these people, Teresa's reform was like a wound that would soon infect the whole organism if someone did not quickly put a stop to it. And someone was about to do just that.

Exterior view of the Carmel of Segovia; drawing by Hye Hoys (1866–1867)

While Teresa was dotting the countryside with her Carmels, the monastery of the Incarnation in Ávila—where she had spent her earlier years of religious life—was threatened with moral and material ruin. Religious observance and the quest for perfection were escaping rapidly through its ever-open parlor doors, while neglect of finances had brought the nuns to a state of near destitution and starvation.

The ecclesiastical superiors, namely, the Carmelite provincial, Father Angel de Salazar, and the Dominican, Father Pedro Fernández, saw the danger of total collapse, but their reaction was to blame Teresa for being the cause of it all. This "blame game" had appeal; it gave them an excuse to put a stop to this "wandering, gadabout" nun's highly successful founding of reformed monasteries.

With apparent respect, they recalled her and made her prioress of the Incarnation. It was the kind of honor she would gladly have done without, but obediently she embraced this heavy cross and prepared to return to the gilded cage.

On October 6, 1572, Teresa returned to her former monastery, to a community that made no secret of its hostility. The glares and generally threatening behavior of close to 200 nuns must have stretched her courage to the limit. Their hostility stemmed from the fact that Teresa had left them to seek greater perfection, coupled with their fear that she would now try and convert them all to the Discalced way of life. But they really had nothing to fear. With one intuitive stroke of genius, Teresa began to break down the barriers. When she arrived, she called them all to the chapter room. There she placed a statue of Our Lady on the prioress's seat and placed her keys beside it, indicating that it was Mary who would henceforth be prioress. Then she sat on the floor at Our Lady's feet and quietly began to reassure the community with the following words: "Mothers and sisters, through obedience Our Lord has sent me to this house to perform this duty. . . . I come only to serve you and to please you in any way I can. I am a daughter of this house and the sister of each one of you. Don't be afraid of how I shall govern, because although I have lived and governed among reformed nuns, by God's goodness I am well aware how those who are not should be governed." (Gracián, *Scholias y addiciones*)

In very little time, the great ship of the Incarnation, which had been taking on water at an alarming rate, was again afloat. It even became a model of religious observance. That it did so was due in no small measure to its prioress's inspired idea of bringing Father John of the Cross as confessor to the community.

For Teresa, this term of office was honorable imprisonment, as we have said. And no matter how honorable it is, a prison is still a prison. The superiors, backed by Rome, saw to it that Teresa could not get out even to attend to pressing problems in monasteries she had founded. Even the Duchess of Alba failed to obtain this permission for her.

But female ingenuity is a very powerful thing. When a woman of Teresa's personality and intelligence sets out to achieve something, there are no walls or other form of defense capable of stopping her. The mother foundress appealed directly to King Philip II himself, and he granted her request immediately.

She quickly made the trip to Alba but would neither eat nor sleep at the castle as she had a convent of her own there. She preferred to go up to the castle daily to give the noblewoman a little of what her fame and riches could not bring her: a little company in the loneliness in which she found herself, with her husband and son away fighting in the Spanish Netherlands, and some comfort too in her grief and worry over the love affairs of her son, Don Fadrique.

While Teresa was in Alba she also settled a family quarrel between her nieces and her brother-in-law, Juan de Ovalle, over who should pave a road near his house.

She returned to the Incarnation as quickly as she could. From then on the visitator proved more amenable to further requests to go out. The nuns in Salamanca took advantage of this improvement to call on Teresa's talent for calming troubled waters. She went down to see if she could succeed in having them moved from the damp and unhealthy house the students had been in to the house they were trying to buy from that shifty couple, Pedro de la Vanda and his wife.

It was in Salamanca on that occasion that the following incident happened to her. Let's listen to Teresa tell about it:

View of Segovia; the majestic cathedral dominates the landscape

One day while I was praying, the Lord told me to go and make a foundation in Segovia. This sounded quite impossible to me, because I couldn't go unless I was told to, and the apostolic visitator had made it clear that he wanted no more foundations. . . . I wrote and told him that, as he knew, I had been commanded by the father general to make foundations whenever the opportunity presented itself: that both the bishop and city authorities of Segovia had given permission for one of our monasteries; that I was willing to go ahead with this foundation if ordered to do so. . . . He immediately told me to make this foundation and sent me a license to do so. I was amazed" (F 21.1–2).

Teresa had good friends in that ancient Castilian city for some time, particularly a family by the name of Jimena, one of whom had become a

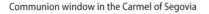

Communion window in the Carmel of Segovia

House where St. Teresa lived in Segovia at the time of the foundation

Discalced Carmelite nun in Salamanca. This was Isabel de Los Angeles, the nun whose singing of the verse "Would That My Eyes Could See You" sent Teresa into ecstasy one Easter morning. She and an aunt and a cousin of hers had often implored Teresa to come and found a Carmel in Segovia; they had even traveled to Ávila to ask her. Requests, permission, and the word of the Lord convinced Mother Teresa to undertake it. And the hope of being thus able to remove her nuns at Pastrana from the machinations of the Princess of Eboli was an added incentive.

"While still in Salamanca, I arranged to have a house rented for us. I had learned from our experience in Toledo and Valladolid that it was better for many reasons to look for a house of our own after we had taken possession. In the first place, I didn't have a penny with which to buy a house. Besides, once the monastery was founded, the Lord would provide for it and then a more suitable site could be chosen" (F 21.2).

Doña Ana Jimena informed Teresa that everything was ready. The bishop, Diego de Covarrubias, had granted his permission. So had the city fathers

Nuns' side of the parlor (speak room) in the Carmel of Segovia

(one of whom was Doña Ana's nephew); and the house was not only rented but furnished as well. Buoyed by that good news, Teresa left Salamanca.

First, she went to Ávila, by way of Alba de Tormes and Medina. From there about the middle of March the founding party of eight set out for Segovia. They included four nuns; Father John of the Cross; the chaplain, Father Julian of Ávila; Antonio Gaytán; and Mother Teresa herself. Here Teresa pauses to introduce readers to Antonio Gaytán:

> He was a gentleman who lived in Alba. . . . I have said who he was, because in subsequent foundations he worked hard for me and was a great help, so he will be mentioned again. If I were to recount all his virtues, I wouldn't finish so quickly. . . . We have been fortunate that the Lord called him and Father Julian of Ávila to this work, though Father Julian, of course, has been with us from the very beginning. It was through such company as theirs that the Lord must have planned so much good to happen to me. (F 21.6)

On facing page:
The tomb of St. John of the Cross above the altar in the monastery church

Wooden bench used by St. Teresa

Then, as if expressing her gratitude to these faithful friends, she adds, "It is well, daughters, that you who read the story of these foundations should know how indebted we are to them; they work hard without any self-interest so that you can enjoy the blessing of living in these monasteries, and you ought to commend them to the Lord and let them at least have the benefit of your prayers. If you only knew the bad nights and days they went through for you, and the hardships they endured on the roads, you would do this most gladly" (F 21.7).

At last they reached the city, deliberately arriving after nightfall. It was the vigil of the feast of St. Joseph. They first stopped at an inn, El Mesón del Aceite, and from there sent word to Doña Ana, who came and took them to their rented house. Everything was so well arranged that Mother Teresa had only to allocate their quarters to everyone and attend to a few minor details.

According to Father Julian, "When we arrived we set up an altar and decorated it. Then we hung tapestries on the walls, placed a bell in one of the windows and at dawn I said Mass and reserved the Blessed Sacrament." To that we can add that a notary certified what had taken place and declared the foundation official. It was the feast of St. Joseph, March 19, 1574. The new monastery was dedicated to St. Joseph of Carmel.

In fact, the nuns had the blessing of three Masses that morning. Father John of the Cross celebrated the Eucharist when the first Mass was finished, and he had just finished when a visitor arrived. Don Juan de Orozco y Covarrubias, the bishop's nephew and prior of the canons regular, happened to be passing by the house. When he saw the porch so clean and decorated he decided to go in and say Mass.

Everything had gone very smoothly with this foundation—so smoothly that Teresa was surprised and somewhat puzzled. But her surprise didn't last long. Wherever you go there are always people who envy the success of others. Segovia was no exception. Soon there were people running to the vicar general to denounce this monastery that had sprung up overnight, complete with altar and bell, nuns, and chaplains.

The vicar general knew nothing of the nuns' arrival, so he stormed in indignantly to see for himself. He angrily demanded to know whose permission they had to do this. The answer that it had been done with the bishop's verbal permission didn't satisfy him. He ordered the altar dismantled and the Blessed Sacrament removed. That brought him face-to-face with the bishop's nephew, who was still saying Mass. The celebrant, however, played dumb. Father Julian hid. The nuns were behind their grille. Poor Father John of the Cross was left to bear the brunt of the attack.

The high-ranking cleric's anger drew no response from this saintly little man. And since his anger was more at their failure to notify him of their arrival than on the question of permission, he gradually calmed down. His earlier threat of putting them all in jail was changed to placing a policeman at the door (no one knew exactly what for). And the threat to dismantle the chapel became a temporary prohibition from reserving the Blessed Sacrament.

Teresa, as usual, remained perfectly calm. As far as she was concerned, it would have been worse if all this had happened before they gained possession. She adapted to the law in force at the time. That is why she became an expert at these quick, stealth strikes when founding monasteries. Her maneuver had military precision: get to the city in question, find the house, have Mass celebrated, and you're home free—or so she thought.

Views of the monastery of St. John of the Cross

As we've already said, the reason Teresa wanted to have a house in Segovia was to provide a refuge for her long-suffering daughters in Pastrana. It was with this goal in mind that she had brought Julian of Ávila and Antonio Gaytán along. Their job was to get the nuns out of Pastrana, which they did. Doing this meant smuggling them out of their convent by night. The rest of the story reads like something out of an adventure novel!

On April 6 or 7, 1574, the nuns and their chaperones finally reached Segovia. The prioress in Pastrana now became prioress of the new Segovia foundation. That was the end of the Pastrana foundation. It had lasted a mere four years and was the only one to fail in Teresa's lifetime.

Teresa herself was not really surprised at the outcome. With only the princess's volatile whim to hold it together, Teresa expected as much from day one. Summing it up herself, she wrote, "In short, the Lord permitted it." No further complaint or ill feeling. Nor apparently did the princess hold a grudge against Teresa or her nuns. Perhaps the woman was no more capable of sustained hatred than she was of steadfast love.

But let's get back to the Segovia foundation. The day came to move from a rented house to one of their own. "We stayed there for a few months until a house had been bought, a proceeding which involved us in several lawsuits." (Legal problems seem to be a perennial ingredient in Teresa's foundational mix!) ". . . Oh, Jesus, how troublesome it is to have to contend with such a variety of opinions! Writing about it, it doesn't seem much; but going through it was plenty of trouble" (F 21.9).

At last, the house was bought, thanks to the influence and money of Doña Ana and her daughter. In fact, both of these ladies were not satisfied with giving the nuns all they had; they both entered the Order as well.

The house was in a street quite close to the cathedral. Too large for its owner, it was nevertheless too small for a community of nuns, especially a strictly enclosed one. The nuns later expanded it, at the expense of a large part of their garden. All that now remains of the original building are a few hermitages; they are really no more than little cells on the second floor, which are now inaccessible, as that floor is no longer used. Teresa used to go up there for some peace and quiet.

This very fervent community was blessed in having St. John of the Cross's company and teaching during the latter years of his life. When the Discalced Carmelite friars established their headquarters in Segovia and introduced the form of government known as the *Consulta*, he was the first councilor. So the nuns of Segovia had the benefit of the last teachings of one of the purest and most learned souls the church ever knew. Two precious letters of his to the two Jimena ladies are still preserved there.

Segovia, then, becomes another point at which these two privileged souls—Teresa and John of the Cross—converged. These twin mystics had a common depth of religious experience, but they were also very different from one another.

St. John translated his experience into poetry; he sang it and distilled it into verses and symbols. Later, he paraphrased his poems and in doing so produced the highest-quality theology. For him, prayer was life with God, a matter of pure faith and love. He was strongly attracted to ever-deeper immersion in the mystery of Christ and to "the feast of the Spirit" that is celebrated in the life of every Christian.

St. Teresa, on the other hand, had so vivid an experience of God that she felt driven to tell people about it. To do so, she needed a group. When she had achieved this, she gave it a characteristic lifestyle, "a little college of Christ," she called it. Then, to teach this group, she wrote. In the background there is always the transcendent God, who is at the same time a dear friend and "so close that there is no need to shout" at him.

It has been said that Teresa was "water and the thirst for living water," whereas John of the Cross was "fire and waiting for the light in the night." He preferred cosmic symbols: fire, night, mountain, light. She chose more homey ones: garden, water, worm, butterfly, castle. The blending of both their gifts gave birth to that particular charism that still enriches the whole Carmelite family.

As if grateful to Segovia, St. John of the Cross left it his mortal remains. They were brought there from Ubeda and are venerated in the friary church that he built.

But let's get on with our story. Teresa's longest journey is still ahead of her, so let's set off once more in her company.

BEAS de SEGURA
St. Teresa's Route from Castile to Andalusia

1574
October

Having completed her term as prioress of the Incarnation, Teresa returns to St. Joseph's in Ávila, her first foundation.

Late December

Teresa goes to Valladolid to settle the case of Casilda de Padilla and her relatives.

1575
January

Teresa plans a long trip: Valladolid, Medina, Toledo, and Beas (Jaén).

January 13

In Medina, Mother Teresa gives the habit to 14-year-old Jerónima de la Concepción, Doña Elena de Quiroga's daughter. The saint dedicates the following verse to her: "Who brought you here, maiden / from the valley of sadness? / God and my good fortune" (P 24).

February 16

After crossing the Guadarrama sierra and the Despeñaperros pass in the middle of winter, Teresa reaches Beas.

February 24

Mother Teresa founds the Carmel at Beas and names Anne of Jesus (Lobera) prioress; she chooses another illustrious nun, María de San José (Salazar), for Seville.

April

Father Jerome Gracián arrives at Beas from Seville en route to Madrid. Teresa pledges obedience to him.

The start of the foundation of the Carmel of Beas, in *The Book of the Foundations:* Chapter XXII: which describes the foundation of the glorious St. Joseph of the Savior in the place of Veas [Teresa's spelling of Beas in the autograph], year MDLXXV, on the feast of St. Matthias."

A Constellation of Teresian Companions

The foundress now had a small retinue of illustrious figures taking part in her movement: Fray John of the Cross and Antonio de Jesús, the pioneers from Duruelo; Jerome Gracián, son of the royal secretary, and apostolic visitor; the Italian Maríano de San Benito, renowned as an engineer; and Juan de Jesús Roca, a Catalan from Alcalá University. Another Italian, Nicolás Doria, a Genoese financier, was soon to join them. Teresa had taken the two most distinguished nuns of the group with her to Beas: María de San José, prioress of Seville and Lisbon and a great writer; and Anne of Jesus, for whom St. John of the Cross wrote his *Spiritual Canticle,* and who later established the Teresian Carmel in France and the Spanish Netherlands (today's Belgium).

# Beas de Segura

ST. JOSEPH'S OF THE SAVIOR

FEBRUARY 24, 1575

"While I was still there," writes St. Teresa, referring to her visit to Salamanca to attend to the move to a new house,

> . . . a messenger came from Beas (in the Kingdom of Jaén). He brought me letters from a lady of that place and from other people asking me to go and found a monastery there, as they already had a house for the purpose. . . . I questioned the messenger and he told me many good things about the place. And he was right, for it really is very beautiful and has a lovely climate. But when I thought of how far away it was, it seemed foolish to go. (F 22.1)

The distance was not the only reason that founding in Beas seemed unwise. Remember, Mother Teresa was in

Salamanca only as a special favor. Her superiors cannot wait to get her back to the Incarnation, where she was prioress. Besides, she knew only too well that the visitator was just as opposed to her looking after the monasteries she had already established as he was to her making any further foundations. Her health too was deteriorating, and the trip in question was more than 365 miles. After all, Beas was a place she had never even heard of. As far as she was concerned, it could have been at the other end of the world. She wondered whether it could still be within the territory of Castile, for she had no permission to found beyond those borders.

But the inner forces driving her to overcome all obstacles were already in motion: her determination to lay down a thousand lives rather than let one soul be lost; her great desire to see one more tabernacle on earth; the thought of how well God would be served in this new house; and finally that blind obedience to her father general, who had told her to lose no opportunity of making a new foundation.

If the opportunity was not taken advantage of, it was not going to be her fault; so, she passed the responsibility for a decision on to her superior.

> I thought to myself that since he (the superior) was in Salamanca at the time, I should make no move until I had consulted. . . . When he received the letters he sent me word that he had been impressed by the devotion of these people and thought they ought not be disappointed. He told me

Drawings by Hye Hoys
(1866–1867)

On preceding page: ruins of the Carmel of Beas in the mid-19th century;

At left: the façade of the church

to write and tell them that if they obtained the permission of their Order, arrangements would be made for the foundation. [Beas was under the jurisdiction of the Knights of St. James of Compostela, at that time known as the military Order of Santiago.] He added that they were certain to be refused . . . but that I should not send them an unfavorable reply. (F 22.3)

So if Teresa was going to play it safe, so was the superior. He didn't refuse, but he was certain nothing would happen. That way he fell afoul of neither the lady from Beas nor Mother Teresa.

Who was this lady from Beas? Teresa tells us:

here lived in this town a gentleman called Sancho Rodriguez de Sandoval; he was of noble lineage and well-to-do. . . . Among the children God had given him were two daughters: Doña Catalina Godínez and her younger sister, Doña María de Sandoval. The older of the two would have been fourteen [fifteen actually], when the Lord called her to Himself [as a nun]. Until then she had no intention of leaving the world; in fact, she had so high an opinion of herself that her father could not find a suitor who she thought good enough for her. (F 22.4)

So here was a teenager with rather high expectations: she had her choice of the most eligible young men from the best families in the kingdom, and they were not good enough. And then the Lord brought about a mysterious change. Her conversion was quite sudden; it happened one day when she read the inscription over the head of the crucified Christ. A simple everyday occurrence like that changed her completely one morning, and the event was accompanied by a mysterious, loud noise that woke up the whole house. It must have had something of "the strong wind" of Pentecost about it, for then and there Catalina emerged in the habit of a *beata* (a woman privately consecrated to God but not a nun) to let everyone see how determined she was to cut herself off from the world.

The change that came over Catalina proved the vision's authenticity. She continued to run the house but now spent most of the night in prayer, since her daytime duties left no time for it.

The Despeñaperros Gorge, the pass from Castile to Andalusia, in the heart of the Sierra Moreno

Her father died four years later, and then God tested her with severe illnesses, but these served only to refine her virtue and strengthen her desire to be a nun. Before long, Catalina's younger sister, Maria, expressed similar desires. After their mother died, both sisters decided to become nuns. If necessary they would establish a monastery like the ones they heard Mother Teresa of Jesus was founding. They had heard about these from a Jesuit friend, Father Bartolomé de Bustamante. Catalina even had dreams in which she saw herself living in such a community.

But there were three apparently insurmountable obstacles to the fulfillment of these dreams: Catalina's poor health, which had kept her bedridden for a number of years in the past; the need to obtain the license from the Council of Military Orders (which never granted such licenses); and the problem of communicating with Mother Teresa and getting her to come to Beas when she was being deliberately tied down where she was.

We've already seen how the last problem was solved. The first too melted away unexpectedly. On January 16, 1574, Catalina was suddenly and completely cured while a Jesuit celebrated Mass in her room before a picture of Jesus being taken down from the cross. As for permission from the knights, it was pointless to even ask them. So Teresa went directly to King Philip II. As soon as he saw the petition was for reformed Carmelites, he immediately granted it. As Teresa wrote later, "Lord, it's easily seen that when You want to, You easily change anyone's mind!"

She promised the people in Beas that she would be delighted to come as soon as she had made the rounds "of certain monasteries." Her superior was rather annoyed at the way things were going, but he could not refuse the permission he had promised. Therefore, when her term of office as prioress of the Incarnation was over, Teresa began recruiting nuns for the distant foundation she was very soon to embark on.

Leaving Segovia, she visited Ávila, Toledo, and Malagón. From there she set out with several nuns, the inseparable Father Julian and Antonio Gaytán, and a secular priest who was later to become a Discalced Carmelite in Beas, changing his name from Gregorio Martínez to Gregorio Nacianzeno (after the great theologian of the Eastern churches, St. Gregory Nazianzen).

Never before had Teresa faced so long a journey, nor had she traveled with so large a party. They left Malagón about the first week in February 1575. In front of them stretched miles of muddy, potholed roads over the never-ending plains of La Mancha. At least the Lord was good enough to bring about a remarkable improvement in Teresa's health, and she had a relatively comfortable journey from that point of view. Down they went to Almodóvar del Campo, passing Daimiel and Manzanares on the way. There is a tradition in Almodóvar that says Teresa shook the dust from her sandals over some unpleasantness she experienced there. Whether the unpleasant experience happened or not, it's definitely far-fetched to describe her shaking dust from her sandals—Teresa never wore sandals. (She and her nuns wore handmade canvas and hemp-rope slippers, called *alpargatas*.)

Chiclana

Panorama of Beas de Segura

Fountain of Villar

Teresa's visit to Daimiel gave rise to an equally interesting if unlikely legend. The story goes that Teresa and her party were guests of Don Miguel Merino Morales. He prepared a banquet worthy of his own generosity, and all held their breath to hear the reaction of a saint known for mortification to a luxurious plate of partridge. Mother Teresa simply tucked in her napkin, allegedly saying, "When it's time for partridge, let's have partridge! When it's time for penance, let's do penance."

Behind these anecdotes, which may or may not be true, there is a common desire to show that Teresa's holiness was spontaneous, unpretentious, and free of gimmickry—the kind of holiness one would expect of a woman who hated pretense and long faces. The object of the stories is not to show her tolerance of human weakness but rather to demonstrate the supreme art in which she excelled: making virtue likeable and attractive.

In Almodóvar they stayed with the parents of a man who was later to reform the Trinitarian Order, St. John Baptist of the Conception. From there they crossed into Jaén through Torre de Juan Abad and Villamanrique and finally reached Beas de Segura.

With lively company, the comments on places more renowned for bandits than anything else must have been rich. But they don't seem to have experienced any danger worth mentioning, except for an incident near a place called Despeñaperros. They took a wrong turn here and, when they realized they were lost, began to pray to St. Joseph. Suddenly they heard the

Façade of the Carmel of Beas

Monuments to St. Teresa and St. John of the Cross in Beas

voice of an old man warning them to stop or they would find themselves at the bottom of a steep cliff. They were sure the warning—which they immediately heeded—came from St. Joseph himself.

Their reception in Beas has been put on record by Father Julian of Ávila:

> The Mother and her nuns were so well received in Beas that . . . the whole town, young and old alike, turned out to greet them with great rejoicing. Outriders on horseback escorted their wagon to the church grounds, where everyone had gathered to meet them. The clergy, dressed in surplices and led by a cross-bearer, formed a procession and thus conducted them to the church with all due solemnity. Afterwards, they were taken to the house assigned to them as a monastery and officially received by the lady who had so long desired and sought to have them. . . . We remained with Mother Teresa . . . until Father Master Jerome Gracián arrived, and then, at his bidding, departed for Seville. (*Vida* II, 8)

On the following page:
High altar in the monastery church

That was February 24, 1575, the feast of St. Matthias. The monastery was called Saint Joseph of the Savior. Here the two Godínez sisters received the Carmelite habit with every sign of the greatest happiness.

We should address two additional topics before concluding this hurried account of the Beas foundation: the presence here of Father Jerome Gracián, then at the height of his fame, and the fact that it was here that Teresa fell in love with the charm of Andalusia.

Although she had heard of Father Gracián and had had some correspondence with him, Mother Teresa had never met him until she came to Beas. Son of the famous humanist secretary of King Philip II, Don Diego Gracián de Alderete, and of a mother of Polish origin named Doña Juana Dantisco, Jerome had no fewer than twenty brothers and sisters, all of them quite talented. Father Jerome himself was an exceptionally gifted man. He had a charming personality and an excellent memory. A handsome man, he was also a talented orator; and most important, he had the tact and patience needed to resolve interpersonal difficulties.

People far less noble or talented gradually succeeded in turning the father general against Father Gracián, especially when he undertook the unenviable task of visitator to both the Calced and Discalced Carmelites of Andalusia on orders from the Dominican, Francisco Vargas. Teresa thought this appointment would enhance the prestige of the Discalced members of the Order. But, fed false information, the general condemned it immediately.

It was to clarify the actual facts of this situation that Father Gracián and Mother Teresa met in Beas. Such was the impression he made on her that she described it in words that she had never dared use of anyone else: "I think he's perfect. We couldn't have asked God for better. I have never seen perfection combined with such gentleness. I wouldn't have missed seeing him and speaking with him for anything" (Ltr 81. 2, F. 23. 7).

Gracián too has left a record of this meeting: "[Mother Teresa] revealed her spirit to me without any reservations, and I did likewise with her. We agreed there and then to proceed in complete agreement in all our undertakings. Furthermore, she took a particular vow of obedience to me, over and above her normal religious vow." (*Peregrinación*, Dialogue 13)

What better opportunity than this to take a brief look at that sublime facet of Teresa's soul called friendship? Friendship for St. Teresa is "pure love," something completely disinterested and self-sacrificing. It seeks to provide the loved one with everything good and to spare him or her everything harmful. Friendship endures across space and time. It's necessary to the point of being indispensable. It is open to and complemented by the divine transcendence, for both friends desire the greatest good for one another, and the greatest and most lasting good is God.

Teresa saw love and friendship as an absolute and irreplaceable value. Perhaps that is why she looked on God, on her Christ, as a good friend, and on community life as a little group of chosen people in which "all must love one another . . . all must be friends" (WP 4.7).

She herself was a very charming, affectionate person, and people found it easy to love her, whether her relatives, brothers and sisters, acquaintances, or later, her nuns. Teresa had always been particularly gifted in this respect, and the passing years served only to develop it, to increase the radius of her love's influence.

Her friendships embraced people at all levels of society: cardinals and bishops, priests and religious, bankers and cattle dealers, adults and children alike. Even platonic love had a place in her heart. We need only recall the admiration and love she expressed when writing to Fray Luis de Granada, though she knew him only from his writings.

Of all the people her heart went out to, Father Gracián was perhaps the object of her greatest friendship. Humanly speaking it was an unlikely friendship: Teresa was sixty at the time, Gracián just twenty-eight. But where friendship joins two spirits, age matters little. It was a shame that so pure a meeting of these kindred spirits would lead to a Calvary of bitter suffering.

It was all due to a mistake. Teresa had the prior general's permission to make foundations, but only in Castile. Neither she nor her advisors realized that Beas was in Andalusia, and thus under entirely different ecclesiastical jurisdiction. To make matters worse, Father Gracián thought that once Teresa was in Beas he could authorize her to found in Seville, since he was visitator for Andalusia.

The famous frogs' pool (in the Beas monastery garden), named for an event in the life of St. John of the Cross

To make a long story short, the Carmelite prior general in Rome listened to the calumniators who were portraying both Gracián and Teresa as rebellious troublemakers and took Teresa's action as an act of defiance. Relations between the Discalced and the rest of the Carmelite Order became strained and led to a great deal of hostility and suffering in the years that followed.

Mother Teresa immediately realized the direction things were going and hastened to explain herself to the prior general, but he didn't listen to her. Because Teresa placed so much value on obedience, the tension this caused must have been a very painful moral trial for her.

Account of the Seville foundation from *The Book of the Foundations:* "Chapter XXIII: which treats of the foundation of the monastery of the glorious St. Joseph of Carmel in the city of Seville. The first Mass was said on the same day as [the feast of] the Holy Trinity in the year MDLXXV."

SEVILLE
Teresa's Route to the Seville Adventure

1575
April–May

At Beas, Father Gracián orders Teresa to make a foundation in Seville.

May 18

Teresa begins the trip from Beas to Seville by way of Córdoba.

May 23

She arrives in Córdoba but has problems entering the city. Mass at the little church of Campo de la Verdad.

May 24

Pentecost Week. The saint receives further intimate graces at St. Anne's hermitage in Ecija.

May 26

She arrives in Seville.

May 29

Foundation of the Seville monastery.

August 12

Two of Teresa's brothers, Lorenzo and Pedro, arrive at Sanlúcar de Barrameda from South America.

November 24

Teresa plans the Caravaca foundation, which is completed in December.

1576
May 27

Teresa moves to the new Seville Carmel.

May 28

She leaves Seville for Castile.

June 23

Teresa arrives in Toledo. Here she learns that orders have come for her to suspend all work on her foundations.

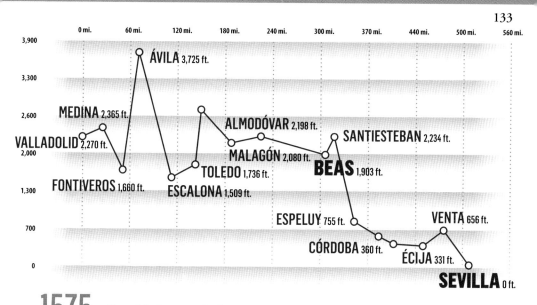

| | 0 mi. | 60 mi. | 120 mi. | 180 mi. | 240 mi. | 300 mi. | 370 mi. | 440 mi. | 500 mi. | 560 mi. |

ÁVILA 3,725 ft.

MEDINA 2,365 ft.

VALLADOLID 2,270 ft.

ALMODÓVAR 2,198 ft.

SANTIESTEBAN 2,234 ft.

MALAGÓN 2,080 ft.

BEAS 1,903 ft.

FONTIVEROS 1,660 ft.

TOLEDO 1,736 ft.

ESCALONA 1,509 ft.

ESPELUY 755 ft.

VENTA 656 ft.

CÓRDOBA 360 ft.

ÉCIJA 331 ft.

SEVILLA 0 ft.

1575 Chart of the journey to Seville

Tried by the Inquisition

Teresa and her nuns face an onslaught of accusations; *The Book of Her Life* is denounced in Castile. In Seville, Teresa and her nuns are accused of the heresy of being *alumbrados*, or illuminists. Don Álvaro de Mendoza hands over the manuscript of the saint's book to the Castilian inquisitors. The renowned Dominican theologian Domingo Báñez defends it before the court (July 7, 1575), but Teresa's work is still held by the Inquisition. In Seville the inquisitors interrogate Mother Teresa, who easily put their suspicions to rest. However, they still order her to write and submit to them two long accounts of her life and mystical experiences (ST 4–5).

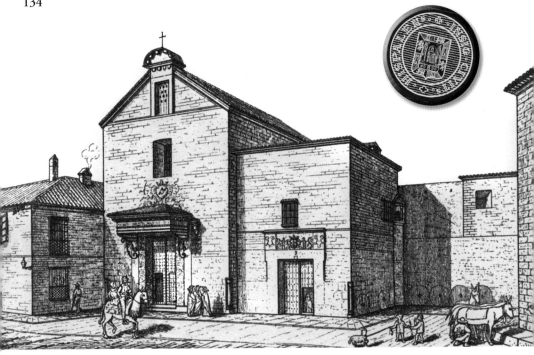

Façade of the Carmelite monastery in Seville; drawing by Hye Hoys (1866–1867)

Seville

ST. JOSEPH OF CARMEL

MAY 29, 1575

"The older she gets, the more she travels," moaned Father Julian on one occasion. And how right he was. When she was younger, Mother Teresa did not look beyond the immediate vicinity of Ávila for opportunities to make new foundations; now that she is old (with shorter life spans in 16th-century Spain, sixty was "older" than it is today) and plagued by persistent bad health, her journeys get longer and longer.

This time the goal was Seville. God knows it was not of her own choosing. Her own reason and the Lord himself told her that this move would mean plenty of trouble, and had she been free to choose she would have preferred Caravaca or Madrid. In fact she had already chosen nuns for the latter. But Father Gracián, who was now her immediate superior, had other ideas, and so she traveled farther into Andalusia.

There was a certain sadness about her departure from Beas; she had a presentiment that she would never be with these sisters again. When she was leaving, she said to the prioress, Mother Anne, "Here, take my mantle! It's new and more suitable for a young person like you. I'll take yours; it's old and worn, so it will suit me fine."

And so she took her leave of this monastery which, through St. John of the Cross's lavish attentions, was later to produce some famous Discalced foundresses. On Friday, May 20, the party set out. Teresa took six nuns, as well as Julian of Ávila, Antonio Gaytán, Father Gregorio Nacianzeno, and a retinue of drivers and mule boys. Teresa had a very high opinion of these six sisters: "They were such that I would have dared to go even to the land of the Turks with them. . . . They had a long way to go, so I made sure they were the most suitable for our purpose" (F 24.6).

The caravan consisted of four covered wagons and very little luggage. Father Maríano had been instructed to have everything ready for them in Seville and had painted a very rosy picture of what they would find there, so why bother to bring any more than just what they needed for the trip? They did bring food, but the heat soon made that inedible; fortunately, Teresa had also insisted on a supply of water.

This journey turned out to be Teresa's longest and most adventurous. All sorts of things happened to them—some funny, others far from it. Let us listen to the accounts the travelers themselves have left us: "For all our hurry, we didn't reach Seville till the Thursday before Trinity Sunday (May 26), and we suffered from the most intense heat on the way. We didn't travel during siesta time, and yet, Sisters, getting into those wagons was like going to Purgatory, for the sun had been beating down on them. Sometimes by thinking of Hell and other times by telling themselves they were doing or suffering something for God, those sisters bore the journey happily and cheerfully" (F 24.6).

The first day they took their siesta in a pleasant forest. There was such an abundance of water, flowers, and birds that Mother Teresa became enchanted at the setting; they had a challenge getting her to leave and get back on the road. That was the honeymoon.

They spent the first night at a hermitage dedicated to St. Andrew, situated a short distance beyond Santistéban. They took turns praying and resting on the cold stone floor. In the cool dawn they moved on toward Linares, fording two rivers on the way. At midday, Father Julian tells us,

> We came to an inn by the roadside. There were some men there, and I had never seen such a depraved lot in all my life. . . . They shouted all sorts of vile things at Father Gregorio Nacianzeno and there was no way we could convince them to stop it. . . . In the end, they drew knives and began fighting among themselves. . . . While all this was going on the Mother and sisters remained in their covered wagons, and were not seen. Had the men seen them, they would have treated them as they had treated Father Gregorio.

And as if that were not enough, he adds, "We were very thirsty in this inn. . . . The heat was unbearable; a cup of water cost two *maravedís*, and each sister needed several. Wine was cheaper than water there." As for food, María de San José tells us that "most days there were only beans, bread, cherries, and things like that. If we found an egg for our Mother we thought it a great thing."

They passed Linares and Alventoso (scene of a famous battle with the Moors) and reached the ferry to cross the Guadalquivir. Here, more adventure awaited them. Father Julian writes, "The boatman cheated us; he said his boat would take us all, but it was fit for only a small number of people and horses. For the sake of a little extra profit he tried to do something which could have cost us very dear." What happened was that one of the wagons broke loose and drifted downstream, nuns and all. Some of the remaining nuns were immediately on their knees crying out to God, while others helped the men to haul on a rope. Fortunately, the prayers were heard and the wagon became stuck on a sandbar. A man who had been watching the proceedings helped them get on their way again.

La Giralda, the bell tower of the Seville cathedral; originally a minaret during the city's Moorish period

The third day, with no worse enemy than the unrelenting sun to contend with, they made good progress.

The fourth day was undoubtedly the worst. Mother Teresa became so ill that they had to seek refuge in an inn. According to Father Julian, "They were given a little room where pigs used to be kept." As Teresa describes it, "The little room was roofed like a shed and had no windows. If you opened the door the sun blazed in. The sun here is not like in Castile—it is much worse. They put me to bed. But I would have been better off on the floor, for the bed was so uneven that I didn't know which way to lie; it was like a bed of sharp stones" (F 24.8). María de San José had a few further remarks to make about this incident: "That was all she [Teresa] noticed; she didn't see all the spider webs and bugs. . . . And then there was the shouting and swearing of the people . . . and the noise of the dancing and tambourines. In the end we decided it was better to take her out of there, so we set off again in the full fury of the early afternoon sun" (*Recreaciónes* 9).

That night they slept outside an inn on the outskirts of Córdoba, rather than face the chaos of an inn.

The fifth day was Pentecost Sunday, May 22, and it began early in Córdoba. Teresa tells us about that morning:

> I found what happened on Pentecost Sunday harder to bear than the things I've mentioned above. We tried to get into Córdoba as early as we could so that we could hear Mass without being seen. We were directed to a church just over the bridge, for greater privacy. But when we went to cross the bridge, we found that the wagons couldn't cross without a permit from the governor. Since people were not up yet, it took more than two hours to obtain the permit, and meanwhile a crowd began to gather, trying to find out who was in the wagons. . . . Then, when the permit finally arrived, they discovered that the wagons were too wide to go through the bridge gate. They [the projecting ends of the axles, actually] had to be sawed off, and that took more time. When we finally got to the church it was full of people, since it was a church named in honor of the Holy Spirit. . . . So there was a solemn celebration and a sermon. . . .
>
> We dismounted from the wagons near the church. Nobody could see our faces because we had our veils down, but the sight of us like that and with our white mantles and *alpargatas* was enough to cause an uproar. . . . As we entered the church a man came up to me and held back the people. I begged him to show us to a side chapel. He did so and closed the door on us. He did not leave us until he had seen us safely out of the church. . . .
>
> You may think this was nothing, Sisters, but I assure you it was one of the worst things I've been through in my life. From the uproar in the congregation one would have thought the church had been invaded by bulls. (F 24.12–14)

On the sixth day they reached the relatively large town of Ecija (population 7,000). Here they were undisturbed as they attended Mass and received

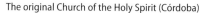

The church of the same name today

The original Church of the Holy Spirit (Córdoba)

the sacraments at their leisure in the hermitage of St. Anne. Mother Teresa spent the day in the privacy of the sacristy, thanking the Holy Spirit for his favors. That day too she made the special vow of obedience to Father Gracián for life.

They were now only fifty-some miles from Seville. But they still had to pass through Fuentes and the somewhat frightening incident at the inn of Andino. Sister Leonor de San Gabriel narrates what happened there: "Near an inn they call Andino Inn, we came on a group of soldiers and muleteers fighting with knives. There was complete disorder, and nobody could make them stop. Mother stuck her head out of the wagon and with one word calmed them all down" (Testimonies of the beatification process, *Sanlucar la Major*, 1596).

They spent the last night at Mairena, a pretty little town with fountains and whitewashed buildings. After Mass at dawn, they were on their way to the Promised Land.

Seville at that time had the largest population of any city in Spain and was at the height of its fame and splendor. It had some 30,000 permanent

Left, Cremona, main gate to the town; *right*, ruins of the Venta de Albino near Cremona

residents. And because it was the main point of departure for South America, it had a large transient population as well. As a port to the Indies, it was a clearinghouse for everyone dreaming of adventure. And since it was also the gateway through which riches to Spain entered and were distributed, it was a mecca for international merchants, soldiers, priests, missionaries—as well as every conceivable kind of rogue.

The Church of Seville was presided over by Don Cristóbal de Rojas y Sandoval, a good friend of Father Gracián's and of the Discalced Carmelites in general. He had given them the much-coveted hermitage of Los Remedios and longed to see Mother Teresa, whom he knew only from their correspondence.

Besides having possibly the most magnificent cathedral in Spain, Seville had no fewer than thirty parishes, as well as numerous chapels. It was also home to eighteen houses of friars and twenty-four convents representing many different religious orders. This was the Seville which Teresa's four covered wagons entered on the morning of Thursday, May 26, 1575. Fathers Gracián and Maríano had painted such a pretty picture of how things would be that Teresa thought she would rest for a few days and then return to Castile.

There was no need to worry about the house; Father Maríano had already rented one. They were bound to be well provided for financially in a city of so much wealth. The usual problem about obtaining episcopal permission did not arise—nobody even mentioned it—because the archbishop was more like a father to them and was eagerly looking forward to meeting Mother Teresa. Father Gracián even had prospective vocations already waiting to join the community.

But then reality hit. They found the house to be "small and damp." It *was* furnished, but they learned that all the furniture had only been loaned for their arrival and most of it was reclaimed almost immediately by the owners. Since the nuns had no friends or acquaintances in the city to ask for help, the money provided by Father Maríano didn't go very far. And on top of everything else, no one had bothered to mention, or had not apparently noticed, that the archbishop was totally opposed to monasteries founded in poverty. What he had been looking forward to was having Teresa and her nuns help him reform the convents of Seville!

Interior of the cathedral of Córdoba, formerly a mosque

That alone might have been reason enough to return to Castile without making any foundation, but there was worse to come. Tension was high between the Discalced and their brethren of the Ancient Observance, the Calced Carmelites. There was internal trouble too. In spite of Teresa's care in the selection of suitable nuns for this arduous undertaking, one bad apple slipped into the basket. After causing untold grief, this nun finally left the Order, but only to continue making trouble. Her lies and slander brought the Inquisition down on Mother Teresa. It had been keeping tabs on her for a while and now decided to conduct a formal investigation into the life of the nuns and every aspect of Teresa's life as well. Whenever Father Gracián worried about the Inquisition's investigation of her *Life*, Teresa would only laugh and say, "I wish they burned us all at the stake for Christ. But don't be afraid, Father. Where matters of faith are concerned, by God's goodness, they will find nothing wrong with us. We would prefer to die a thousand deaths" (*Peregrinación*, Dialogue 13).

The old "Calle de Armas" (Street of Arms), site of the first house in Seville where St. Teresa and the nuns lived

The first few months of her stay in Seville were indeed difficult ones for Teresa. So much so that at times her renowned courage failed her. "No one could have foreseen," she confesses, "that in a wealthy city so full of rich people there would be less help forthcoming for a foundation than in any place I've been. I don't know if it's the climate of those parts. I've always heard it said that the devil has a freer hand there for tempting people, and I was certainly sorely pressed by him. I have never seen myself so weak and cowardly in all my life as I was there" (F 25.1).

Fortunately, the Lord gradually undid the knots in which they were so terribly tied up. After several petitions from Father Maríano, the archbishop finally allowed Mass to be offered in the house on Trinity Sunday, May 29, provided they avoided any type of solemnity. After that he frequently sent one of his chaplains to say Mass for the nuns and to ask about Mother Teresa. Finally he paid them a visit himself and, as Teresa wrote to Antonio

Entrance and courtyard of the original monastery

Gaytán, "he did what I wanted." In fact, the archbishop's attitude toward the Carmelites did a 360-degree turn: he later gave them wheat, money, and other gifts, and showed the nuns and others that he had deep respect for them.

Outstanding benefactors now began to come forward. The names of people such as Doña Leonor de Varela, a cleric named Garciálvarez, and the saintly prior of the nearby Carthusian monks will always have a place in accounts of the founding of this monastery.

The sky was completely cleared of its threatening clouds with the longed-for arrival of Teresa's brother Lorenzo from South America. At his own expense he solved the last of their problems: the purchase of a house.

Lorenzo had been in Ecuador for several years and had done very well for himself, rising to the post of mayor of Quito. Lorenzo had sent her money on several previous occasions, including for her very first foundation in Ávila. Now he was home, with his children—Francisco, Lorenzo, and Teresita. His brother Don Pedro de Alumada had come with him too, but a third brother, Jerónimo de Cepeda, had died in Panama shortly before they were due to embark.

What a joy it must have been for Teresa to embrace her loved ones after so many years and to see her nephews and the pretty nine-year-old Teresita for the first time. Her charming little niece would provide her with many enjoyable times in these latter year of her life. (To fast-forward a little in our narrative, Teresa was on her way from Burgos to Ávila to receive Teresita's profession when she became seriously ill on the way and died in Alba de Tormes.)

How often Teresa had dreamed of the Americas! That was where all her brothers were, and she kept in constant touch with them. Now, most of them were dead.

The "New World" had made an impression on Teresa in several ways. She kept hearing about the millions of souls who had not heard the Gospel, those "Indians," stories of conquest and evangelization, and of exploitation too. "Those Indians cost me dearly," she once wrote in a letter to Lorenzo. "America"—how much more immense it was than anyone had ever thought!

The Americas occupy a much larger place in Teresa's books and her whole outlook than they do in those of John of the Cross. Yet the latter died

Embossed silver cover that for several centuries held the original manuscript of St. Teresa's *Interior Castle* (Carmel of Seville)

just when he was being sent to Mexico. Some people—not her superiors but the evil tongues of mischief-makers in Andalusia—would have liked to send Teresa too, to Mexico, or any other continent, for that matter!

Everything that came from the Americas enthralled Teresa: potatoes, which were to do so much to alleviate hunger in Europe; native medicines with fascinating names; and above all, coconuts. When they sent her one from Seville to Toledo, trying to get it open turned into quite a community event!

Proof of the impact that the New World made on Teresa is evident in the various objects from it that are still cherished in her Carmels, especially in Ávila and Seville.

When all the initial opposition and trials were over, the people of Seville quickly came to love both Teresa and her daughters. Vocations flourished. And in her free moments, Teresa loved to watch the royal fleet in the port, where there were always ships sailing for or returning from "America."

Teresa believed in thinking big and aiming high. Her concern took her throughout Europe as well as the New World. She was always praying for

The white mantle worn by St. Teresa, among the relics treasured by the Seville Carmel

Europe, with its wars in the Low Countries and Portugal and France, the widespread religious strife, and the seemingly endless political upheavals.

But to return to something more pleasant, at long last, Teresa's Discalced Carmelite nuns had a house of their own. It was situated in the Calle de Zaragoza, in the parish of St. Mary Major, close to the magnificent Franciscan monastery. Today the Seville city hall stands in its place.

The new monastery was inaugurated and blessed on June 3, 1576, and dedicated to St. Joseph of Seville. The event followed the now-usual pattern: Mass, procession, and general rejoicing. The archbishop reserved the Blessed Sacrament and then, at her request, gave a public blessing

Silver and crystal reliquary symbolizing "the interior castle;" it holds the autograph of the book

to Mother Teresa. To her consternation, however, the archbishop—who appreciated her spiritual stature more than most—then insisted that she bless *him*, also in public. Though considerably embarrassed, she complied with his request.

We cannot end our account of Seville without mentioning that the two most faithful portraits we have of St. Teresa—one a painting, the other a word picture—date from this time. The first was made by a brother whom we've already met at Pastrana, Fray Juan de la Miseria. Father Gracián commissioned the portrait, but it shows more goodwill than artistic merit. Teresa agreed to sit for it only under obedience. The story goes that when it was finished she groaned, "May God forgive you, Brother John, for making me so ugly and bleary-eyed!" The second portrait comes from firsthand knowledge of the saint; it's drawn with love and reverence, enshrined in the following beautiful lines by María de San José:

> The Saint was of average height, maybe a little more. In her youth she was
> known for being very beautiful, and one could see to the very end that

The original manuscript of St. Teresa's *Interior Castle* in the Seville Carmel

she really was. Her face was rather unusual, being neither round nor oval. Her forehead was high, smooth, and very beautiful. Her eyebrows, dark brown rather than black, were wide and a little arched. Her brown eyes were round and sparkling; they were not very large, but they were very well set. Her straight nose narrowed toward the top, and neatly met the eyebrows, forming a pleasing bridge between them. Her nose was round and somewhat flat, the nostrils small and arched. The nose as a whole did not protrude very much from her face. . . . Her mouth was well-proportioned, the upper lip straight and thin, the lower thicker and slightly protruding. It was graceful and prettily colored. . . .

On the whole, she was more inclined to be stout than thin, but very well-proportioned. She had small but lovely hands. On the left side of her face there were three moles, rising in a line from just below the left side of her mouth. (*Recreaciónes,* 8)

Very soon all that Seville would retain of St. Teresa would be these two portraits and a host of precious memories.

Once she had seen her daughters safely settled in their new home, she said goodbye to them on June 4, 1576. Ten years later, thanks to the generosity of Don Pedro Cerezo Pardo, they moved to the monastery they have occupied ever since. This benefactor's only daughter, Doña Catalina, entered the Order in 1618 and brought with her Teresa's most famous work, *The Interior Castle*. Father Gracián had made a present of this treasure to her father.

Today this book, protected by an artistic reliquary, is the Carmel of Seville's most prized possession. There are other relics and memorabilia still preserved here as well: a substantial *collection of letters;* part of the saint's *little finger;* the *white choir mantle* she wore; one of her *alpargatas; Fray Juan's portrait of her;* and various other objects connected with St. Teresa and this foundation.

What remains, above all, is Teresa's cheerfulness. Her own charm and wit have blended with those of the Andalusian temperament to make of this community a worthy witness to the woman for whom "a sad saint was a sad sort of saint."

Drum and drumsticks used by St. Teresa during recreation with the nuns, recalling her very human playfulness (Carmel of Seville)

CARAVACA
St. Teresa's Route: A Foundation from a Distance

1575
March

St. Teresa sends two representatives, Julian of Ávila and Antonio Gaytán, to Caravaca to negotiate the foundation.

June 9

King Philip II intervenes to remove obstacles to the foundation.

July 19

Teresa writes to the king to thank him for his help.

November 24–25

Mother Teresa and Father Gracián authorize the nuns to make the foundation.

December 18

The founders' caravan arrives in Caravaca.

1576
January 1

The Caravaca Carmel is officially established. Teresa names Ana de San Alberto (later a distinguished disciple of St. John of the Cross) as prioress.

The Caravaca foundation as described in *The Book of the Foundations*: "Chapter XXVII: treats of the foundation in the town of Caravaca. The Blessed Sacrament was reserved on the first day of the new year in MDLXXVI. It is dedicated to the glorious St. Joseph."

Historical Background

The years 1575 to 1581 are turbulent ones for Teresa. In Piacenza, Italy, the general chapter officially opposes her work (1575). In Seville she is ordered to remain enclosed and stop any new foundations, under threat of excommunication.

In Ávila, John of the Cross is arrested and imprisoned.

A new papal nuncio, Felipe Sega, comes to Madrid from Rome. He condemns Gracián and denounces Mother Teresa as "a restless gadabout of a woman, disobedient and obstinate." (Ltr 269.3)

At the same time, the Inquisition seizes Teresa's most important book, her *Life*, and closely monitors her activities and behavior.

It is against this background that she travels from Seville to Toledo (1576) and from Toledo to Ávila (1577). And still against this stormy background she writes her masterpiece, *The Interior Castle* (Toledo-Ávila, 1577).

The outcome is eventually favorable: in March 1581, Teresa's new Discalced Carmelite family obtains its independence, with its own superiors and legislation.

1576

The route of St. Teresa's return trip to Castile

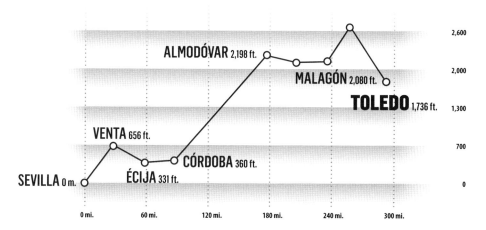

Caravaca

ST. JOSEPH'S MONASTERY

JANUARY 1, 1576

This is a very old town. In the 3rd century BC, Ptolemy referred to it as Carca; it later became Caravaca. Under Arab rule, Caravaca was in the kingdom of Todmir; later, it even had a king of its own. After it had been taken back from the Moors, Caravaca was given to an uncle of King James I. Then it passed into the hands of the Knights Templar, and in Teresa's day Caravaca belonged to the military Order of Santiago, also known as the Knights of St. James of Compostela.

According to a popular guide book, "[Caravaca] is situated on a pleasant plain, has good walls, old-style towers, and is dominated by a strong castle. The surrounding countryside is fertile in bread, wine, olive oil, honey, fruit, silk, and hemp, as well as being good for cattle and hunting. It has a population of about 600 people" (*Alcazar de Sevilla Guide Book for Sightseers*).

A small number of people played a prominent role in our story, among them Don Alonso Muñoz, a member of the Council for the Indies; his wife, Doña Catalina de Otalora; and Don Rodrigo Moya and his wife, Doña Elvira Caxa.

Doña Catalina lost her husband. Shortly afterward three young women from the nobility (all named Francisca and all related) heard a sermon by a Jesuit that so moved them they decided to become nuns. Doña Catalina knew all three of them; one was her niece and another the daughter of a friend. She agreed to have all three young women come to live with her. Since Caravaca had no convent, she promised to help them establish one. On the advice of the Jesuits, they decided to invite Mother Teresa of Jesus to advise them on founding a monastery like hers.

Teresa received their invitation when she was in Ávila. She has told us herself how it affected her: "When I saw the desire and the fervor of those good people and considered how far afield they had to go in search of Our Lady's Order, I was quite moved and I wanted to help them realize their good intention. I was told the place was near Beas, so I took more nuns with me than I would otherwise have done . . . with the intention of going on to Caravaca when the Beas monastery had been founded. But as the Lord had decided otherwise, my plans were of little use, as I've said when speaking of Seville" (F 27.2).

When Teresa reached Beas she learned that Caravaca was not as close as she had thought. She was also told that the roads were impassable. If that were the case, she reasoned, confessors and superiors would have considerable difficulty visiting the nuns; that cooled her enthusiasm somewhat. Still, she had given her word, so she sent Father Julian and Antonio Gaytán off on a fact-finding mission.

The two men set off across what is now the province of Albacete to that of Murcia, where Caravaca is located. They were guests of Don Rodrigo Moya, the father of one of the young women. In the meantime, one of the girls had changed her mind, and Doña Catalina did not have enough money for the project. But the impression made on Teresa's two scouts was so favorable that the necessary papers for the foundation were signed before they left the town. "They left the ladies very happy, and returned well pleased with both ladies and the place itself . . . though not so pleased with the roads" (F 27.4).

With the agreement drawn up, one part of the venture was completed. There was, however, another end still to be tied up, so to speak: the permission of the military Order of Santiago. This time the problem was a little different from that encountered in Beas. The knights were willing to authorize the foundation—but only on condition that the nuns would become subject to them. Teresa was going to have none of that.

The extensive social and political influence that these half-monastic, half-military institutions wielded in 16th-century Spain was one of the lingering vestiges of the Middle Ages. St. Teresa certainly was not going to allow her nuns to become the subjects of these people, however well-meaning or powerful they were. Faithful to her Order, she was determined that whatever she founded was going to be under obedience to the father general, Juan Bautista Rubeo, who had clearly requested her to establish her new monasteries "within the Carmelite Order."

This was not the first time she had to hold firm to her commitment that her Carmels would be under the Order. Not long before, Teresa had been offered a foundation in Valencia by the archbishop himself. But she refused because he made it a condition that the house be subject to him.

Ironically, while Teresa was doing her utmost to be loyal to the father general, he and the Order's general chapter had just condemned her. She was ordered to cease all founding activity and to retire to a monastery—it was literally a form of house arrest.

However, she did not know of that decision yet, and her reaction to the obstacle placed in her way by the knights was to appeal to the king himself, as she had done in other crises. Philip II settled the matter quickly. He made an exception for her but added that the nuns were to pay tithes to the Order of Santiago and acknowledge its right to give permission. With the control of the knights reduced to specific and limited monetary matters, Teresa was

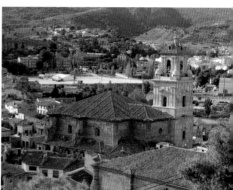

Alcazar Shrine of the Holy Cross in Caravaca

A view of Caravaca

happy and wrote once more to thank the king. Once more too, she urged her daughters not to tire of praying for him.

This was not the first letter Teresa wrote to King Philip II, as we have already seen; nor would it be the last. He was her court of appeal in all serious issues. Thus, she wrote asking his support when she wanted the Discalced to become a separate province within the Carmelite Order. She wrote to defend Father Gracián when he was defamed and persecuted. She called on him for justice when Father John of the Cross was imprisoned in the Toledo monastery. This latter, indeed, was perhaps the strongest and most daring letter she ever wrote.

We have alluded several times to certain "tensions among the friars." It may be well here to quote some lines from that great historian of Carmel, Father Silverio de Santa Teresa:

> As always happens in such cases, the reform which Teresa so opportunely undertook was evaluated quite differently by different people at first. They were not to know the fruit which it would, in time, bear in the church. It is not surprising, therefore, that the Calced Fathers should have had some misgivings about it and even opposed it. Apart from some excesses, which are inevitable whenever feelings run high, Calced and Discalced proceeded with the best of intentions, and God made use of the struggle between

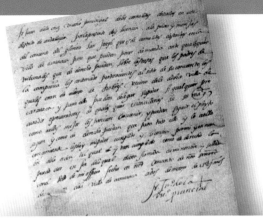

An original letter written by St. John of the Cross

them to purify the virtue of their holy foundress and make the Reform more vigorous. When the long and exhausting storm was over, the Reform came out of it strong and buoyant. Calmly evaluating those events today, it is easy to excuse both sides for what they did.

But to return to Caravaca, by the time the problem of the permission had been solved, Teresa was on her way to Seville. She and Father Gracián agreed that since she could not go personally, the nuns would have to make the journey without her. They were accompanied by two Discalced fathers and the faithful Father Julian and Antonio Gaytán.

So, for once, Teresa had to write about what she heard rather than what she saw: "When they arrived, the people received them with great joy. . . . They founded the monastery and reserved the Blessed Sacrament on the feast of the Holy Name of Jesus (January 1), 1576. Immediately afterwards, both girls took the habit" (F 27.9). The monastery was dedicated to St. Joseph.

It was the first time a nun other than Mother Teresa took charge of a foundation. Caravaca's on-site foundress was Sister Ana de San Alberto from Malagón. In fact, Teresa would never see Caravaca, but it had a special place in her heart. It was also one of St. John of the Cross's favorite communities. He visited it several times, and it is one of the few Carmels that have preserved the letters he wrote them.

The town of Caravaca still proudly displays Teresa's original agreement in its municipal archive. One interesting sign of Teresa's affection for the Caravaca Carmel and, indeed, for the traditions of the town, is the devotion she displayed from then onward for their famous relic of the true cross,

Entrance to the Carmel of Caravaca

better known as the Cross of Caravaca. She carried a reproduction of it with her for the rest of her life, and it was found between the sheets of her death-bed when her body was removed.

This fact merits a few words on Teresa's love of symbols such as this one. She was always a lover of images and symbols. Her faith in such things—in this case the Cross of Caravaca—was not some kind of fetishism. They were concrete representations of a mystery, and Teresa's use of them was

Statues of Our Lady of Mount Carmel and St. Joseph which St. Teresa sent to the Carmel of Caravaca

not latching on to something superficial but a reminder of something profoundly religious. Take, for example, Teresa's approach to Christ. Even here her symbolist approach is in evidence, whether in the form of the cross or the marriage symbols of the Song of Songs.

Then too there is the way she understands the soul as a castle and as a garden. It was as if she carried within herself both the strength suggested by the one and the fruitfulness of the other. Life itself, especially that of the spirit, is expressed in terms of two beautiful symbols: the silkworm destined to be transformed into a butterfly; and water, giving life to all it touches, welling up in the inner fountain of the soul and flowing through every human action into every undertaking. And finally, the symbolic mystery, which she made so much her own, of the struggle between water and fire. The water she receives from Christ; the fire she has within herself—"great desires" and the inner drive to do more and more.

Reliquary of the Cross of Caravaca

Teresa probably thought of such things when she held her little Caravaca cross. According to tradition, the cross's origin was a vision that the slave priest Ginés Pérez had during the Arab domination of Spain. Later, as an artifact, this cross is alleged to have converted the Moorish petty king Abu Zeit. The original Cross of Caravaca was eventually stolen. What the city treasured in Teresa's time was a replica containing a relic of the true cross of Jesus, which the pope had sent to comfort the townspeople on the loss of their treasure.

VILLANUEVA DE LA JARA

St. Teresa's Route in the Lands of Don Quixote

1580
June 25

Teresa travels to Medina and Valladolid.

June 30

Further trips from Valladolid to Medina, Alba, and Salamanca.

November

Teresa sets out from Salamanca to Ávila; from there she goes to Toledo and then Malagón. She arrives in Malagón on November 24 and immediately begins directing building work on the new monastery.

1581
February 13

Teresa leaves Malagón, accompanied by the founding nuns. She stops at Roda (17–19), at the Socorro hermitage, where Catalina de Cardona had lived.

February 21

She arrives in Villanueva de la Jara.

February 25

She gives the habit to the founding nuns.

March 18

Teresa injures her left arm again, this time with the winch of the

well. She had earlier broken it in Ávila on December 24, 1577.

March 20

She leaves Villanueva de la Jara for Toledo. When she arrives on March 26 she is seriously ill.

June 7–8

Teresa travels from Toledo to Madrid and then Segovia, arriving on June 13.

July 6

From Segovia to Ávila.

Early August

Teresa travels from Ávila to Medina and Valladolid. In Valladolid she becomes very ill with the famous epidemic of "universal catarrh," today's severe bronchitis.

Historical Background

Teresa: Teresa's health by now was extremely fragile. She suffered once again from problems with her left arm, which had been out of action for several months in 1578. She fell ill at the end of the journey back to Toledo and caught the summer epidemic of severe bronchitis that ravaged Castile that year. As a result her strength was severely reduced.

Her work and her followers: The storm was blowing over, and the foundations resumed. On May 5, Father Gracián's reputation was restored, and he was reinstated to his duties. Juan Bautista Caffardo was elected as the Order's new prior general on May 21. On June 22 with the papal brief "Pia Consideratione," Pope Gregory XIII grants the status of autonomous province to Mother Teresa's Discalced Carmelite friars and nuns.

The political scene: The cardinal-king Henry of Portugal died without a successor. The Portuguese proclaimed Antonio, prior of Crato, king. However, Philip II of Spain was the closest claimant to the throne. War broke out between Spain and Portugal. In November 1580, Philip sent the Duke of Alba with Spanish armies to invade Portugal and claim the throne for Spain. The previous summer (July 22, 1579), Teresa had written a distressed letter "against war" to Don Teutonio de Braganza.

Account of the foundation in *The Book of the Foundations:* "The foundation in Villanueva de la Jara. After the foundation in Seville was finished, there were no more foundations for four years. The reason for this was the beginning of the sudden tremendous persecution against the . . ."

Villanueva de la Jara

ST. ANNE'S MONASTERY

FEBRUARY 21, 1580

With the founding of the Seville monastery [which came after Caravaca, though it is described before it] there were no more foundations for over four years. This was because of the great persecution to which both male and female Discalced were suddenly subjected. There had been some before, of course, but never as bad as this; it almost put an

Exterior view of the Carmel of Villanueva de la Jara; drawing by Hye Hoys (1866–1867)

"This is how the saint traveled;" a modern reenactment of her arrival in Villanueva de la Jara

end to the whole undertaking. It showed clearly how the devil felt about the holy beginning the Lord had accomplished, and that it was really His work, for it had made considerable progress. The Fathers, especially their leaders, suffered greatly from the almost total opposition of the Calced Fathers. (F 28.1)

How calmly and briefly St. Teresa dismisses this truly bitter parenthesis! This zealous female conquistador had been confined to barracks until further notice. Her energies, however, would thrive by remembering what had been accomplished. For the moment, at least, she would turn them inward to only become stronger. The mother foundress was not ordered to seclude herself in any monastery in particular, but the one she chose was Toledo. Perhaps her friendship with the postmaster of the city prompted this move, because for the foreseeable future she was going to have to conduct all her business by mail. Or she may have been attracted by Toledo's good climate, which was so beneficial to her poor state of health.

She devoted most of her time in Toledo to writing. She produced a veritable flood of letters, continued her work on the *Interior Castle* and the *Foundations*, and wrote a brief work for the friars and nuns on how to conduct the visitation of Discalced Carmelite monasteries. She also dreamed. She relived those beautiful days in her first foundation at St.

Joseph's ("the most restful of her life") and the interminable travels that followed. While Teresa is under "house arrest," so to speak, let's take a closer look at those travels.

Like St. Paul, Teresa was one day impelled by the Holy Spirit to *go . . .* to take to the road and tell of what she *had seen and heard.* She needed the journeys to launch her testimony and establish her conquest: a new tabernacle, and more souls who loved and praised their God.

For many of Teresa's contemporaries, clerical and lay, it was a scandal that a woman—a cloistered nun and supposed champion of reform at that—should spend most of her time on the road. In fact, this was probably the single most disconcerting thing about her. Her superiors took her to task for it, as did two successive nuncios, Nicolás Ormaneto and Felipe Sega. The former was Teresa's friend and did it gently—through Father Gracián. But the latter, influenced by the Calced opposition, was quite harsh about it. To Sega we owe the famous (or infamous!) description of her, cited earlier, as "a restless gadabout of a woman."

Even Teresa's biographers were not too happy about this aspect of her life. Francisco de Ribera, for example, devotes a whole chapter of his biography to explaining why she had to travel as she did. Simple people didn't understand either. One day Teresa, to make conversation with one of the muleteers, told him she was traveling to earn her reward in heaven. Somewhat taken aback, he replied that he could get to heaven from home and didn't need such complications.

Yet, one of the most characteristic features of this "gadabout" was that she took her lifestyle with her when she traveled. Here is Gracián's account of what it was like to travel with her:

> I want to describe now how she traveled; I accompanied her quite a lot and to many places.
>
> Usually, three of us religious and some laymen accompanied her. Before we arrived at an inn, she would send one of us ahead to order food and reserve rooms. One of the latter had always to be sufficiently large to allow all the nuns to stay together. Everything they would need had to be

Parish church of Villanueva de la Jara

put in that room, so that they wouldn't have to ask for anything and the maids would have no reason to go in there. . . .

They always lowered their veils when they left the wagon, and the first thing we always did, if it was the right time for it, was to attend Mass, at which the Saint would receive Holy Communion.

Once in their room, she closed the door and appointed a doorkeeper, just as if she were in a monastery. Very often she was ill, and since the sisters couldn't go out to the kitchen, one of us did the cooking. This amused her greatly, though the sisters would have been happier if they could do more for her. . . .

Sometimes the rooms had no doors. Then she would place us outside to ensure that no one could come in. In some inns the nuns were not able to have a room to themselves. We would then bring in some blankets and hang them to form a screen so that the nuns would always have privacy.

That way, the nuns could ring their little bell for periods of silence, personal prayer or the Divine Office, as they did in the wagon, just as if they were in their monastery.

The solicitude [of Mother Teresa] for the needs of those who traveled with her was remarkable. One would think she thought of nothing else. . . . Sometimes she spoke so charmingly to those who accompanied us on foot that they forgot their weariness.

At times we traveled on muleback, riding along and chatting about godly things; she rode as well and as steadily as if she were in a carriage. Once, her mule became frightened and bolted. She brought it under control herself, with no screams or other expression of female panic.

And so the time passed—reminiscing, writing, and praying—until at last that happy day came when she was permitted to resume her travels once more. Four years have gone by, and she is now "a little old woman," to use her own expression. Besides, she has lost the use of her left arm ever since the devil threw her down the stairs in Ávila. But she still has enough energy and drive to take to the roads once more, though from now on she would always be accompanied by her faithful nurse and secretary, Sister—now Blessed—Anne of St. Bartholomew.

She began by visiting most of her monasteries: Medina, Valladolid, Alba de Tormes, Salamanca, Ávila, even as far as Malagón. Needless to say, she was received with open arms and great joy everywhere, after an absence that had been as painful as it was long.

Petitions were pouring in from all sides for her to come and make foundations—calls from Zamora, Madrid, Valencia, Lisbon, and others. But the Lord did not direct her to these great places. He pointed to the little village of Villanueva de la Jara, a haven of peace set in the fertile plains of the province of Cuenca.

The background for this choice is closely connected with the famous penitent Catalina de Cardona, who lived in a cave just fourteen miles from Villanueva. Her incredibly ascetic life was bound to have some influence on the people of the surrounding district. Thus it was that some young women of the village were fired with her enthusiasm and cloistered themselves in a house by St. Anne's shrine. It was really a house of *beatas,* but they were determined to make it an austere monastery. They read the works of St. Peter of Alcántara and Fray Luis de Granada for guidance, observed enclosure, and supported themselves by the work of their hands.

Catalina's spiritual directors were the Discalced Carmelite fathers of nearby La Roda and were well known in Villanueva de la Jara for their preaching. This made the Carmelite Order a fairly obvious choice when the above-mentioned young women looked for an Order they could formally enter.

Façade of the old Carmelite monastery in Villanueva de la Jara

The community's refectory

The Communion window

This is how Teresa describes the events leading up to her decision to found there: "When I was in Toledo in 1576 after founding the Seville monastery, a cleric from Villanueva de la Jara brought me a letter from the local council desiring to negotiate with me about receiving into one of my communities nine women who were living together in a shrine" (F 28.8).

Her first reaction was to turn the proposition down flat: Villanueva was too far away from the other foundations; resources seemed insufficient; people accustomed to a particular lifestyle would have difficulty adapting themselves to the Carmelite Rule; they didn't have a house of their own; and Teresa had not met them. As she said herself, "I had been told that they were very good, but since I hadn't seen them myself I didn't know if they were suitable for what we expect of people in our monasteries. So I decided to drop the idea entirely" (F 28.9). Nevertheless, as was her custom, she postponed a final decision until she had consulted some learned man, her confessor, and God on the subject.

Sculpture of St. Teresa outside the church

Meanwhile, during the ensuing time of persecution, the request was repeatedly renewed with ever-increasing urgency. The prior of the nearby community of La Roda joined in the chorus, as did her old friend Father Antonio de Jesús, now also a member of that community. As nearly always happened, the final push came from the Lord himself: "One day just after Holy Communion I was raising up this matter before the Lord, as I had often done before . . . and His Majesty took me severely to task. He asked me what kind of treasures I had needed to accomplish what had been done up to then, and told me to have no doubts about accepting this house. It would render Him great service and benefit souls, He said" (F 28.15). Mother Teresa had been in Malagón about two and a half months when this happened. She was very sick but set out anyway on an eighty-five-mile trip. She left Malagón on February 13, 1580, with the two La Roda friars already mentioned.

Their passage through the intervening villages was like a triumphal march. The villagers knew the friars and had often heard them extol Mother

Teresa's virtues. Now, they turned out en masse to greet her. They vied with one another in hospitality, they entertained her, and they even brought their cattle out for her to bless. The friars of La Roda came in procession to greet her and persuaded her to stay with them for a few days. No wonder her health showed a marked improvement! They reached Villanueva on February 21, the first Sunday in Lent. Teresa describes their arrival:

> The whole municipality and several other people, including Doctor Ervías [the parish priest] came out to greet us. We went first to the village church, which was quite a distance from that of St. Anne. Such was the joy of the whole village that I was greatly comforted to see them receive the Order of Our Blessed Lady in that way. We could hear the bells pealing long before we reached it. When we entered the church they intoned the *Te Deum.* . . . After that they placed the Blessed Sacrament and a statue of Our Lady on two portable platforms, and we set out in solemn procession with crosses and banners. . . . As there was quite a distance to go, they had set up altars at various points along the way, and stopped from time to time to recite something about our Order. We found it very devotional . . . and were moved at seeing so much attention paid to seven poor Discalced nuns for God's sake." (F 28.37)

The new foundation, then, was inaugurated on the day of their arrival; it was dedicated to St. Anne.

Teresa showed so much consideration and affection for these *beatas* that they never forgot it, and the memory of her beneficial influence during the month she stayed there lingered among the villagers as well. One day someone came during recreation time asking to see Mother Teresa. When the nuns expressed some irritation at this interruption that caused her to leave them, she said, "My recreation is to comfort the afflicted." The afflicted in this case was a poor woman whose babies had all been stillborn. Mother Teresa gave instructions that her cincture, the leather belt from her habit, be given to the woman. From then on many women found in St. Teresa's belt a remedy for problems with pregnancy and delivery.

The well in the monastery courtyard, dating back to the time of St. Teresa

Visiting this old monastery today one can still see parts of the original buildings, though their function has changed. The parlors are the ***original hermitage***, which Teresa divided into a chapel and choir. The present sacristy and the turn area is where the ***nuns' living quarters*** were formerly located. The old ***well and winch*** where a mason once accidentally hurt Mother Teresa's arm are still there. And the nuns today treasure a ***statue of the Child Jesus***, "***el Niño Fundador***" (the Child Founder), that Teresa presented to them as a gift.

PALENCIA St. Teresa's Route on the Way to Palencia

1580
Summer–Autumn

Teresa is sick for a long time with the nationwide epidemic of "universal catarrh," a very resistant strain of bronchitis. In her own words, it leaves her "old and weak." But as soon as she recovers, she embarks on the next foundation.

December 28

Teresa sets out from Valladolid for Palencia.

December 29

She opens the new Carmel in Palencia but continues looking for a suitable house for it.

1581
February

Preparations for the decisive "chapter of separation" are completed at Alcalá.

Early March

Opening of the chapter at Alcalá. Mother Teresa follows its news attentively from Palencia.

March 4

Father Gracián is elected provincial of the Discalced.

April 9

Gracián grants Teresa a license and permission to make the foundation in Burgos; however, it will be delayed.

May 26

The Palencia Carmel moves to its new permanent monastery.

May 29

Teresa leaves Palencia, destination: Soria.

The foundation of the Carmel of Palencia as described in *The Book of the Foundations:*
"JHS, tells of the foundation of St. Joseph of Our Lady of the Street in Palencia, in the year
MDLXXX, on the feast of King David."

A Nun of the Order of Carmel

Mother Teresa belonged to the religious family officially known as "the Brothers of Our Lady of Mount Carmel" founded as a group of lay hermits in the early 13th century on Mount Carmel in the Holy Land. Shortly after being established, the Order emigrated to Europe.

Teresa became a Carmelite at the convent of the Incarnation in Ávila, founded in 1479. She lived there for twenty-seven years as a nun (1535–1562) and three years as prioress (1571–1574).

In 1562 she founded a new branch of Carmelites. She saw the new Discalced ("shoeless") Carmelites, nuns and friars, receive permission to become a separate province in 1581. However, it was not until after Teresa's death that it became a canonically autonomous religious family.

Several leading Carmelite friars assisted the saint in the work of her reform and her foundations: the prior general of the Order, Juan Bautista Rubeo (Rossi), who however withdrew his support around 1575; the provincial for Castile, Angel de Salazar, who later gave testimony at the proceedings for the saint's beatification; John of the Cross, a pioneer member of the group of Teresian Carmelites; and Jerome Gracián, who was the group's first provincial and the most deeply identified with the person and philosophy of the foundress.

Palencia

ST. JOSEPH OF OUR LADY OF THE STREET

DECEMBER 29, 1580

View of the Carmel of Palencia in the 19th century; drawing by Hye Hoys (1866–1867)

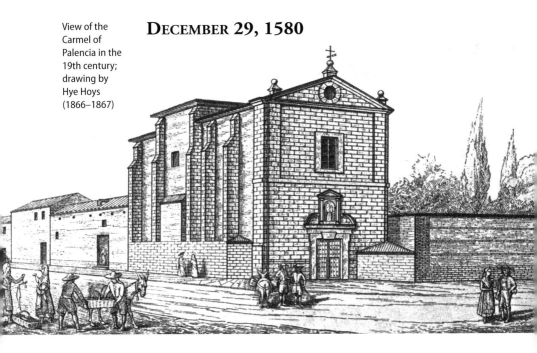

Back in Toledo once more after her triumphal visit to Villanueva de la Jara, Teresa met with Father Gracián. The two sat down to plan the fulfillment of one of Teresa's most cherished ambitions: to make a foundation in Madrid.

Speed is often a characteristic of God's servants; they realize they must do a lot because there is so much to do and it must be done quickly for life is so short. So Teresa and Gracián set to work very quickly. Teresa assured him that a house and money would be forthcoming and that she had already trained her cousin Inés de Jesus to be prioress. All that was missing was the permission of the archbishop of Toledo. Regardless of the obstacles involved, they would obtain an audience with this august personage, Cardinal Gaspar de Quiroga y Vela. All went smoothly. The Cardinal Primate of Spain and its colonies, who was also the Grand Inquisitor, received them on the feast of Corpus Christi. He couldn't have been kinder to them, and they left his presence full of enthusiasm.

According to Gracián, the cardinal was delighted to meet Mother Teresa, as he had been wishing to do so for some time. He assured her that, if she so desired, she could count on him as a chaplain. He recalled the unfortunate fact of her *Life* being sent to (and languishing with) the Inquisition. They had carefully examined it, he said, and decided that it contained safe and profitable teaching; in fact, he had read it himself from cover to cover. The required permission to publish it was granted very readily. The cardinal asked Mother Teresa to pray for him.

But—God's ways again!—as Teresa would have said. In spite of having all they needed, Teresa would not live to see a Carmelite monastery in Madrid.

She now went on to Segovia, where she learned of the death of her beloved brother Lorenzo. It was a painful loss but tempered by the hope of her faith. But Lorenzo's death now meant that her most immediate need was to attend to his three orphaned children. Additionally, the influenza epidemic of that year carried off several of her closest friends as well.

After visiting Ávila and Medina, Teresa herself became seriously ill in Valladolid. She had been sent there at the request of the bishop of Palencia, Don Álvaro de Mendoza, the man who as bishop of Ávila had helped her start the reform and had been a close friend ever since. "Our Lord laid it on his heart that a monastery of our Order should be founded there too. When I reached Valladolid, I fell so gravely ill that they thought I would die" (F 29.1).

Not that another illness was anything new to Teresa; to a greater or lesser degree, she was always sick. Her spirit may have dwelled in heavenly places, but her body was slowly breaking down. This is one more instance of physical limitations putting a brake on her reforming drive. This time it was more serious, however, and it is worth our while to pause a moment and think about it. It was probably this constant struggle with the weakness of her own body that prompted Teresa to leave such a wealth of descriptions of various illnesses and complaints throughout her writings, and so many words of advice on the care of the body. In fact, she mentions so many specific cures that there is a sizeable amount of literature on her medical knowledge. Unfortunately, that too is a subject we cannot enlarge upon here. But let's return to the saint's bedside.

She recovered slowly, but this time it took a lot out of her. Father Gracián noticed the change—she was tired and, for the first time, looked her age. "I was so weak," she says, "that I even lost that confidence which God always gave me when I was starting a new monastery. Everything looked impossible to me" (F 29.3). But they kept after her to make the Palencia foundation: she owed it to Bishop Mendoza, they said—"they" being the prioress of Valladolid, Maria Bautista de Ocampo, and Teresa's onetime confessors Fathers Ripalda and Báñez. Their importunings, even their efforts to encourage her, were of no avail. And then one day all that changed: "One day, after Communion, when I was full of doubts and undecided about either of the foundations (by this time Burgos was being spoken of as well), I beseeched our Lord to give me light so that I would do His will.

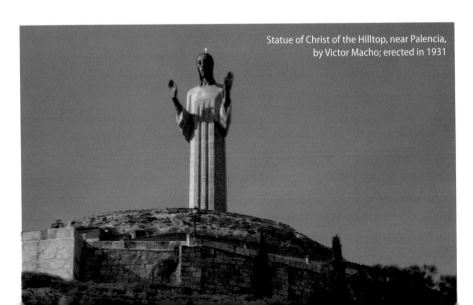

Statue of Christ of the Hilltop, near Palencia, by Victor Macho; erected in 1931

Statue of Our
Lady of the
Street

That desire did not leave me, notwithstanding all my weariness. The Lord said reproachfully: 'What are you afraid of? When have I let you down? I am now the same as I have always been, so be sure to make both foundations.' O great God, how different are Your words from those spoken by men!" (F 29.6).

Suddenly, Mother Teresa was her old self again and lost no time in getting things moving. In his autobiographical book *The Pilgrimage of Anastasius*, Father Gracián takes up the story: "She sent me to take a look at the place and report on the lie of the land, for she was a woman who liked to be well-informed about everything before undertaking a foundation. I went to Palencia and was somewhat discouraged by the priests of the cathedral there: it was a poor town, they said, and the nuns would not be able to support themselves. I was returning with my mind made up not to make that foundation, when I met Suero de Vega . . . an important and very spiritual man. . . . He gave me great encouragement and afterwards helped the monastery generously" (*Peregrinación*, Dialogue 13).

Having received Gracián's favorable report, and a letter from Canon Jerónimo Reinoso placing himself entirely at her disposal, Teresa set a date for the foundation: they would leave on December 28 and, since it was only thirty-one miles away, would inaugurate the new monastery the following day. They set out as planned, but since their route followed the courses of the Pisuerga and Carrión rivers, they soon encountered a fog so dense that at times they couldn't even see one another.

Six nuns accompanied Mother Teresa, as well as the Valladolid chaplain and an admirer named Don Agustin de Vitoria. It was just as well that the journey was short, for between the rigors of the winter and the freezing fog they were chilled to the bone by the time they reached Palencia. Fortunately, Teresa had sent word of their arrival and asked Canon Reinoso to have everything ready for them. The kind priest had done exactly as he was told: food, a warm fire, and beds were all ready. The house, located in the populous La Puebla part of town, had a fine doorway with a magnificent arch above it, set in a beautiful stone facade.

The next day—at that time the feast of King David, of whom Teresa was an ardent admirer—the first Mass was celebrated and the community installed in the new monastery.

The whole city reacted to this new Carmel with considerable enthusiasm. Bishop Mendoza was the first to visit the nuns. He was concerned about their welfare and gave instructions for a supply of bread to be delivered to them daily. The city's *corregidor,* a magistrate appointed by the king, had only reluctantly consented to the nuns' coming in the first place. But now he joined in the general acclaim with a phrase that has become famous: "Mother Teresa must have within her some authorization from the Royal Council of God, which makes us do whatever she wants—whether we like it or not!"

Later, with the help of Canons Reinoso and Martin Salinas, Teresa bought a chapel dedicated to Our Lady of the Street and some houses adjoining it. The community moved there during the octave of Corpus Christi 1581. (They stayed only ten years, however, because the building was too small for the community and also because Canon Reinoso offered them his own house.) Unfortunately, the nuns had spent all the money they

Cathedral of Palencia

had left on remodeling the first building. And like the citizens of the town itself, they suffered extreme poverty there. Relief eventually came with the entrance of a wealthy novice, Doña Luisa de Aragón, whose family fortune solved all the community's financial difficulties. At a later date, the Palencia community moved again, this time to the outskirts of town on the Burgos side, which is where they are today.

Teresa's decision to settle in the hermitage where there was a shrine to Our Lady of the Street is a perfect reflection of another of her leading concepts: that she lived in the Blessed Virgin's house. She always thought of her Order and each Carmel in it as being Our Lady's family. This Marian devotion went back to her childhood, in particular to the death of her mother when Teresa was only thirteen. Her reaction to the loss of her mother was to run to the picture of Our Lady of Charity and tearfully ask Mary to be her mother. "Though I was rather naive, I think my prayer was heard, because

Drum and castanets used by St. Teresa for recreation during Christmas celebrations (Carmel of Palencia)

The saint's distaff

I was conscious of finding this sovereign Virgin as soon as I commended myself to her" (L 1.7). Teresa's life is filled with other examples of her devotion to Mary:

As she left the Incarnation for St. Joseph's, Teresa effectively made herself "discalced" as she began the reform: she took off her shoes before Our Lady's shrine in the crypt of the Church of San Vicente.

Later, as we've seen, when she was named prioress at the Incarnation, Teresa placed the keys in the hands of a statue of Mary and told the nuns the Blessed Virgin was the real prioress.

She felt Mary near in many of the visions with which Our Lord blessed her.

In Villanueva de la Jara, Teresa rejoiced at seeing so many people honor "Our Lady's habit."

Her last foundation would be dedicated to Mary's family, and of course, wherever Jesus was honored with a statue or picture in one of her convents there was bound to be one of Our Lady nearby.

Nor was Teresa's connection with the Blessed Virgin purely external. Mary was part of her interior life, experienced within the context of her

The convent of San Bernardo,
the saint's first residence in Palencia

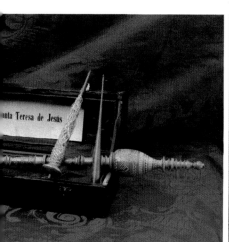

mystical experiences. The mysteries of Mary's life, especially her suffering in union with her Son and her glorification, had special significance for Teresa and left their mark on her teaching.

Some of all this, indeed maybe more than this, must have passed through Teresa's mind as she took possession of the little hermitage of Our Lady of the Street in Palencia. A great grace she received while staying there also had something to do with her love for Mary. It was here she received the *papal brief,* "*Pia Consideratione,*" *separating the Discalced from the Calced*, a document by which Pope Gregory XIII, claiming to have been enlightened by the Blessed Virgin, finally made peace between the two branches of the Carmelite Order.

Relics of Teresa's passage through Palencia include: an *ablution bowl* (for the priest to wash his fingers after Communion), a *coif* or *toque* (part of the Carmelite nuns' habit), two *chairs* (one for indoors, of walnut; the other, a travel chair), a *tambourine* and *castanets,* the abovementioned original copy of the *papal brief "Pia Consideratione,"* which she ordered to be incorporated in the community record book, and many other objects she had or used.

SORIA St. Teresa's Route from Palencia to Soria

1581
May 29

Teresa and her group of nuns set out from Palencia for Soria.

June 2

They arrive in Soria, where Bishop Alonso Velázquez is waiting for them.

June 3

The Carmel of Soria is established.

August 16

Teresa begins the return trip from Soria to Ávila.

August 23

She arrives in Ávila.

September 4–5

Mother Teresa spends the night at Villacastín, weary and "well tired of walking."

September 6

She arrives at St. Joseph's in Ávila; on September 10 she is elected prioress.

November 28

John of the Cross arrives in Ávila, eager to take Mother Teresa to start the Granada foundation. He doesn't succeed; she is already preparing to make the foundation in Burgos instead.

November 29

John of the Cross leaves Ávila for Granada, without Teresa.

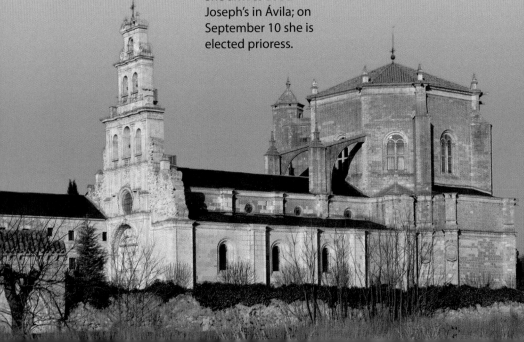

Account of the foundation in The Book of the Foundations: "Beginning of the foundation of the monastery of the Holy Trinity in the city of Soria. It was founded in the year MDLXXXI. The first Mass was said on the feast of our Father St. Eliseus [Elisha]."

The Great Traveler's Interior Landscape

In 1531 Teresa wrote her last introspective piece, *Spiritual Testimonies* 4, addressed to Don Alonso Velázquez, bishop of Osma and Soria. It was like a spacious balcony looking out over the rich landscape of her soul.

From 1560 onward, a powerful inner call compelled Teresa to undertake regular pauses to study her own inner state. Her efforts were recorded in a series of brief, intimate texts called the *Spiritual Testimonies*. Sixty-five are extant, a collection of real jewels.

The last vista was unsurpassable: Teresa experienced absolute peace on her soul's horizon. She was now awaiting her arrival on the final shore.

1581

The Journey to Soria and return to Avila

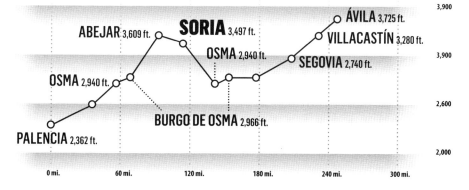

Soria

MONASTERY OF
THE BLESSED TRINITY

JUNE 14, 1581

View of the
Carmel of
Soria; drawing
by Hye Hoys
(1866–1867)

It's said that as Teresa traveled toward Soria she said, "Daughters, when we get to Soria, which is the end of the world, there must be no turning back; you must go on working for God." The phrase "Forward by all means, but nobody must turn back!" became an insistent refrain.

Teresa knew too much about faraway places to think the world ended at Soria. What she was referring to surely was that the end of the road was in sight for her. And she wanted to make it clear to her nuns (and friars) that they must not stop when she was gone; "always forward" must still be their motto.

Teresa really intended to go on to Burgos once the necessary modifications had been made to the hermitage of Our Lady of the Street in Palencia. Writing to Canon Reinoso she even mentioned likely sites for such a foundation. But as often before, God's ways and Teresa's plans didn't always coincide.

God had a way of putting people in her path to help her, people to whom she had reason to be grateful. One of these now asked her to bring her nuns to Soria. He was Don Alonso Velázquez, a learned and holy priest who had helped her greatly with encouragement and advice in the difficult days at Toledo. He was now bishop of Osma-Soria and engaged in the reform of religious life in his diocese. If she would only come to Soria, he had a noble lady who would give all the help they needed. Just let him know, and he would send for her, he said.

Teresa couldn't refuse a friend like Don Velázquez. It would be nice sharing with him again about spiritual matters. And in the process she would add another decade to her living rosary of Carmels. So the usual foundation machine was set in motion: consultation, recruitment, travel.

The prioress chosen for the new monastery was Catalina de Cristo from the Medina Carmel. Father Gracián was unimpressed, to say the least; the woman was barely literate. "Never mind," said Teresa, "she loves God a great deal, is very holy, deeply spiritual, and she doesn't need any more than that to govern properly." Another nun from Medina, two each from Salamanca, Segovia, and Palencia, and Mother Teresa was ready. She also asked Fathers Nicolás Doria and Eliseo de la Madre de Dios to come along.

The journey proved a welcome change in Teresa's state of health. Doña Beatriz de Beaumont—who was financing the foundation—sent a carriage to fetch them and her chaplain, Father Francisco de Cetina, to wait upon their needs. The bishop sent a servant and the sheriff of Corona to make sure everything was in readiness at the inns along the way. Nor was the bishop of Palencia going to be outdone in generosity; he instructed the cathedral bursar to see the party had all they needed for the journey. The weather obliged, the company was pleasant, and the terrain was flat. In fact, the only cloud hanging over the event was the absence of Father Gracián.

Looking back on this trip in a letter, Teresa recalled that "though journeys generally tired me out, that from Palencia to Soria was like an outing. It was a smooth journey and much of it close to rivers, which I loved." There were no fewer than six rivers in that area, and with Teresa's love of water, they must have lightened her heart considerably.

After stopping the first night at Encinas de Esgueva, the following day they reached Aranda and then crossed into the Diocese of Osma. The sheriff was on home ground now and threw his weight around a bit. Teresa was highly amused at his antics yet grateful for his ability to secure the best treatment for them. Apparently not everyone was amused at the sight of a police official escorting the party. At one stop the local people misread the situation and berated the poor man, thinking he was dragging the group off to the Inquisition!

Another anecdote about this trip concerns the faith of the country folk in Teresa's powers of intercession with God. They asked her to obtain much-needed rain for their crops. Moved by their distress, Mother Teresa began to recite the Litany to the Saints with her companions. The downpour started immediately.

Historic Premonstratensian Monastery of Santa Maria de La Vid (of the Vine), on Teresa's route to Soria

On May 30 the group stayed overnight at the guesthouse of the great Premonstratensian (Norbertine) monastery of Our Lady of the Vine. The next day they reached the little walled town of Burgo de Osma. The bishop's residence was there, but he had gone ahead to await their arrival in Soria. The population, some 300, stayed indoors; apparently just then there was a plague scare and nobody was taking any chances.

One more night on the road, stopping at the Hermitage of Our Lady of Velverde. Then at last Soria lay before them, its extensive and imposing walls clearly visible from afar. There had been a time when these walls held a population of almost 8,000; now there were fewer, but the city still had some fine houses.

The party reached Soria about 5 p.m. and was immediately escorted by a mounted guard of honor and greeted by cheering crowds. "The lady who was our foundress was waiting at the door of her house, which was where the monastery was going to be. We were relieved to be inside, for there was a great crowd around us. . . . The lady had seen fully to our every need" (F 30.8).

Entrance to the Carmel of Soria   Entrance to the monastery church

Doña Beatriz de Beaumont, or Beaumonte as she is sometimes referred to in Spanish, was descended from the kings of Navarre and was a daughter of the captain general of the Imperial Guard. According to Teresa, she was kind, generous, penitent, and a great servant of God. Widowed with no children, she spent her whole fortune on works of piety and on her relatives. Two years after the Soria Carmel was founded, Doña Beatriz helped generously with that of Pamplona. At sixty she entered that monastery herself and lived there another seventeen years. With a woman like that Teresa had no difficulties over contractual details. In fact, she reminded her sisters on numerous occasions to treat her with great love.

To return to our story, only a few facts need to be added. The official opening took place on June 14, 1581, the feast of St. Elisha, with the monastery dedicated to the Blessed Trinity. Teresa tells us that the bishop himself celebrated the first Mass and a priest of the Society of Jesus preached the sermon (see F 30.9).

The bishop also donated a church next door and had a covered passage built to connect it with the monastery. This and other projects were completed by August 5, at that time the feast of the Transfiguration of the Lord, an event that was also celebrated with due solemnity.

Among the reasons that Teresa liked the idea of going to Soria, we mentioned that she looked forward to being able to discuss spiritual matters with Dr. Velázquez. She was now able to do so with all the freedom and devotion she enjoyed in his presence and which she speaks of at length in the chapter dealing with this foundation. She told him of the "uninterrupted intellectual vision" of the Trinity and the humanity of Christ she now experienced, and how this mystical grace was compatible with her busy life. She spoke of the tremendous peace it brought and of the full awareness it gave her of God's presence in her soul. We don't know what the saintly bishop had to say to all that. What emerges from her side of the conversation is the sense that this exceptional woman had arrived where the way of prayer is meant to lead. She had reached her destination.

Yet there had been a time in her life when Teresa, destined to be called "Mother of the Spiritual Life" and to be the first woman to be declared a

Arches from 12th-century monastery of San Juan de Duero

Doctor of the Church, was a failure in prayer. But she picked herself up again and discovered authentic Christian prayer through experience rather than books. Through her determination to be stopped by nothing, whatever it might cost, she reached that spiritual fulfillment in which we now see her.

What really set her on the path was the discovery that prayer was communication between friends, frequent conversation with One who we know loves us. It is the ability to relate on a personal level with the transcendent God, to treat him as a friend who is close enough that we can share with him our worries and problems, our very lives.

Where prayer was concerned, Teresa was a disciple before she became a teacher. Her long and deep experience of it was worth a thousand treatises. She was convinced that prayer, like so many other things, was best learned by getting down and doing it. When Teresa teaches, therefore, she speaks from experience. She had encountered the difficulties; knew

Church of Santo Domingo (St. Dominic)

how humility and self-denial helped; was familiar with the stages one went through; knew that prayer was the only door to the interior castle at the center of which God dwells; and knew that true prayer transformed one's life and developed with it. After all, prayer and life are the measure of one another.

Today we live in a world in which we've succeeded in establishing contact with the stars, a world hungering for the widest communication possible, eager to pass beyond cultural barriers to study languages and symbols, and demanding 24/7 communication with our electronic devices and social media. And yet we are practically illiterate when it comes to the one language we really need to know, prayer. Only when we are convinced that prayer is essential to really communicate with God, to discover the inner world of our spirit, and to help humankind will we try and learn how to do it. If we take Mother Teresa as our tutor, it will simply mean learning our native language.

When her presence was no longer needed at Soria, Teresa returned to Ávila via Segovia. On the trip back she had few traveling companions and found the return journey as hard and painful as the initial one had been enjoyable.

The monastery she left behind has changed but little since Teresa's time. Among its mementoes of those bygone days it treasures are *The Virgin of the Five Towns,* a gift to Teresa from Dr. Velázquez; the *old safe, called the ark of the three keys* because it required three separate keys to open it; a *dining room table;* and a few other treasured objects dating back to the time of the foundation.

Gold doubloon, a gift of the saint to Diego de Yepes, her future biographer

Window through which St. Teresa spoke with Doña Beatriz de Beaumont

GRANADA
Fray John of the Cross's Route from Ávila to Granada

1581
June 28

St. John of the Cross is in Caravaca (Murcia).

In the following months he visits several different cities in Andalusia.

Mid-November

John of the Cross travels to Ávila. He goes over with Teresa the plans to found a convent in Granada but is forced to leave without her.

November 28

The last conversation between the two saints. Fray John sets out for Andalusia. He and Teresa will not see one another again.

First half of December

John arrives in Beas, accompanied by the two future foundresses of the Granada Carmel.

1582
January

John and the two nuns travel from Beas to Granada.

January 19

The trio arrives in Granada.

January 20

The monastery is established, but only in a temporary setting.

May 30

St. Teresa writes a long letter from Burgos containing instructions for the prioress at Granada, Anne of Jesus.

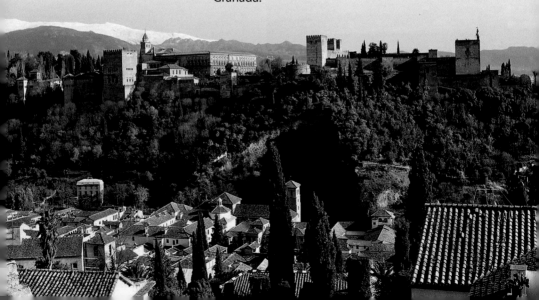

Autograph of a
letter of St. John
of the Cross
with his signature

Two Masters of the Spirit, Teresa of Jesus and John of the Cross

Theirs was a unique relationship: they were both teacher and disciple, reciprocally.

When the two met at Medina in 1567, Mother Teresa was almost 52 years old, Fray John only 25. She had already defined her life and call: she was a Carmelite and a foundress. The young friar was still searching, drawn alternately to the Carthusian Order and Carmel. Teresa promised him he would find what he was looking for in Carmel; she recruited him and trained him to be her great partner in the work of the Discalced reform.

Four years later (1571–1572) as prioress of the Incarnation, Teresa entrusted the spiritual direction of the monastery and its many nuns to Father John of the Cross. The mother foundress herself became his disciple. She was never to reject his teaching. In fact, she confirmed his authority when John became a spiritual director for the Andalusian Carmels: Beas, Granada, Caravaca, and Seville.

After Mother Teresa's death, Father John of the Cross was one of the first theologians to recognize and recommend her spiritual teachings. He proclaimed this explicitly in his *Spiritual Canticle* (stanza 13.7), referring to her books and urging that they be published as soon as possible.

On the following page:
Cloister courtyard, Carmel of Granada

Granada

MONASTERY OF ST. JOSEPH

JANUARY 20, 1582

The Carmel of Granada has the distinction of being the only one in Teresa's lifetime that she never had the opportunity to visit, nor did she describe it in her *Foundations.* She had two eminent people to take her place, however: John of the Cross and Anne of Jesus (Lobera).

Teresa had been back in Ávila about ten weeks, ironing out some problems there, when John of the Cross arrived with a petition to make a foundation in Granada. Some devout people in the city had promised to make enough

Exterior view of the Carmel of Granada; drawing by Hye Hoys (1866–1867)

money available to the vicar provincial of Andalusia to cover all expenses. It was a very tempting offer, especially when presented by someone as beloved and holy as John of the Cross.

But this time Teresa felt she should go ahead with the plans that were already made for Burgos. Thus, she delegated Fray John of the Cross and Sister Anne to make the foundation in her place.

As usual, the best-laid plans went awry. The promised help did not materialize, and the bishop refused permission. Undaunted, the party proceeded to Granada, only to discover that the man who had agreed to rent them a house changed his mind when he found out that it was to be a convent. Fortunately, John of the Cross was spiritual director for a holy widow there, Doña Ana de Peñalosa. If she hadn't taken them into her house, they could well have found themselves on the street.

Anne of Jesus decided to go and see the bishop again. By one of those wonderful events of Providence, the poor man happened to be frightened out of his wits the day she called. A lightning bolt had narrowly missed his bedroom the night before. He took the hint, so to speak, and promptly gave his permission.

The foundation was inaugurated in Doña Ana's house on January 20, 1582, and dedicated to St. Joseph. It was another six months before the nuns were able to rent a house of their own. But then several wealthy young women entered; with the help of their dowries, the community was able to buy the former palace of the Duke of Sesa.

Among the relics treasured in Granada today are some *fragments of St. Teresa's flesh*, her *handwritten renunciation of the Mitigated Rule*, her *cross* and *walking stick,* and the *cell* where Teresa appeared to Anne of Jesus just after her death and restored her to health.

On the following page:

A nun in the Granada Carmel holds St. Teresa's walking stick, one of the monastery's major relics of the saint

BURGOS St. Teresa's Route: Burgos, the Last Task

1582
January 2

St. Teresa leaves Ávila, accompanied by Father Gracián.

January 4

They reach Medina; a brief respite.

January 9

They arrive in Valladolid; a four-day rest.

January 14

The pair leaves for Palencia and stays there more than a week.

January 24

Mother Teresa and Father Gracián leave Palencia and head toward Burgos.

January 25

They reach Burgos at nightfall.

February 23

Teresa and her nuns set up house in the Hospital of the Immaculate Conception.

March 12

The community buys the Mansino house.

March 18

Mother Teresa and the nuns move into the new house.

April 14

Catalina de Tolosa deeds the donation of the Burgos convent to the community.

April 18–19

The archbishop grants permission; the Carmel of Burgos is founded.

May 7

Gracián says goodbye to St. Teresa. This is the last time they will see one another.

May 23

The Arlanzón River overflows its banks and floods the new convent.

July 27

St. Teresa leaves Burgos.

Late July

Teresa is in Palencia.

August 20

Teresa arrives in Valladolid.

September 15

Teresa leaves Valladolid for Medina, arriving September 16.

September 19

Mother Teresa leaves Medina. On orders of Father Antonio she does not go on to Ávila as planned but heads instead for Alba where her presence has been requested by a benefactor.

September 20

She reaches Alba de Tormes at night; exhausted, she goes straight to bed.

October 4

Around 9 p.m., St. Teresa dies in Alba. The Gregorian calendar goes into effect that day, adding 10 days, making her date of death October 14.

Foundations of Discalced Carmelites Made during St. Teresa's Lifetime

Monasteries of nuns (17): Ávila, Medina, Malagón, Valladolid, Toledo, Pastrana, Salamanca, Alba de Tormes, Segovia, Beas de Segura, Seville, Caravaca, Villanueva de la Jara, Palencia, Soria, Granada, and Burgos.

Monasteries of friars (13): In Spain: Duruelo-Mancera, Pastrana, Alcalá de Henares, Altomira, La Roda, Granada, La Peñuela, Seville, El Calvario, Almodóvar del Campo, Valladolid, and Salamanca; in Portugal: Lisbon.

1582

The final journeys: to Burgos and Alba

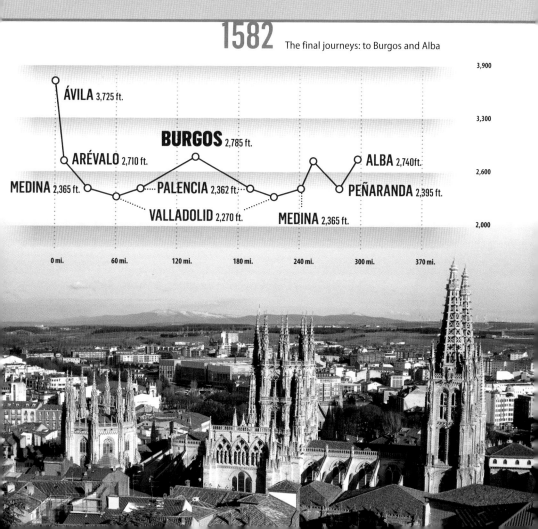

ÁVILA 3,725 ft.

BURGOS 2,785 ft.

ARÉVALO 2,710 ft.

ALBA 2,740 ft.

MEDINA 2,365 ft.

PALENCIA 2,362 ft.

PEÑARANDA 2,395 ft.

VALLADOLID 2,270 ft.

MEDINA 2,365 ft.

3,900

3,300

2,600

2,000

0 mi.   60 mi.   120 mi.   180 mi.   240 mi.   300 mi.   370 mi.

The autograph account of the Carmel of Burgos as told in *The Book of the Foundations:*
"In this chapter we begin to describe the foundation of the glorious St. Joseph and St. Anne in the city of
Burgos. The first Mass was said on the XIX day of the month of April, octave of Easter of the Resurrection,
in the year MDLXXXII."

Exterior view of the Carmel of Burgos; drawing by Hye Hoys (1866–1867)

Burgos

MONASTERY OF ST. JOSEPH AND ST. ANNE

APRIL 19, 1582

We now reach the thirty-first and last chapter of the *Foundations,* Teresa's lengthy account of her last adventure, written about the end of June 1582, just a few months before her death. Teresa doesn't number her chapters but declares that she will "begin to discuss the founding of the monastery of the glorious St. Joseph and St. Anne in the city of Burgos." Nowhere do we find the slightest hint of a tired pen. Quite the contrary in fact; it is a lively tale full of conflict and drama. Three stages stand out: the planning of the undertaking, the apparently inextricable knot of complications, and the happy ending.

In this account Teresa appears for the last time. Without meaning to, she describes herself: her body is extremely frail, suffering from the cold, but her spirit is still on fire and driving it on. She is vigorous and firm. Even when events cause Father Gracián to be out of sorts, no difficulty gets her down. Nor does she let the initiative slip from her grasp. It is she who is the foundress. She may have to direct operations from her sickbed, hardly able to speak with a sore throat, but she does the directing. And that means attending to a lot more than immediate arrangements. She maintains continual contacts with the friends and supporters of this venture. She writes to the bishop of Palencia, urging him to intervene. The day she receives confirmation that a house has been bought, she writes to Lisbon, where the king, the nuncio, and the Duke of Alba were convened at the time (or Teresa thought they were; in reality, Philip II had not yet left Madrid), to obtain permission to have Mass celebrated in this new Carmel. (She has been having a great deal of trouble extracting this permission from the archbishop of Burgos.)

When all the work is done, more writing awaits her: the final pages of the *Foundations.* These pages are packed with the most extraordinary handwriting: no erasures, no sign of hesitation. Just a slight trembling in her hand, perhaps, but still showing all the vigor of youth in those slightly upward-slanting lines. The content too shows complete clarity of mind. Father Gracián himself couldn't have described the foundation better.

What characterizes her account of the Burgos foundation most of all, however, is the interweaving of the divine and human elements. Here God is at once the leading character and a spectator. His words to her are passed on to us with no trace of self-consciousness on Teresa's part: sober words, spoken at the right moment, without any suggestion that they are extraordinary. God's presence is taken for granted, his words recorded as if his speaking were the most natural thing in the world.

So we reach the beginning of the end. "For more than six years, some very senior men in the Society of Jesus, learned and spiritual men, had been telling me that Our Lord would be well pleased to have a house of our Order in Burgos. Their arguments in its favor made me, too, desire this. But the trials which the Order was enduring and other foundations gave me no opportunity of doing so" (F 31.1). So little opportunity did she have, in fact, that she very nearly didn't get to either of her most cherished goals, Burgos and Madrid.

If Madrid was attractive because it was located close to the Spanish court, where so much business had to be done, Burgos had the distinction of being a great and famous city. It boasted many members of the nobility and had the reputation of being very "Christian," with an unusually high number of charitable institutions.

In Teresa's day, Burgos had lost much of its ancient splendor, but it was still the most important city in Old Castile. It had a population of about 8,000, among them some of very noble lineage and not a few wealthy merchants.

To quote a description dating from the days of El Cid, "It was a large city divided in two by a river, each part having its own walls. Strong and wealthy, it had large commercial enterprises, markets, wheat exchanges, and warehouses." In the 16th century it still had the two walls, and its inhabitants had the name of being the most refined, honorable, and hospitable people in the whole of Spain.

The spiritual needs of its population were served by thirteen parishes, as well as famous abbeys, a university, and numerous religious houses of various clerical and monastic religious communities, including Franciscans, Augustinians, Trinitarians, Mercedarians, and others. St. Teresa experienced great difficulty in getting a foothold in Burgos, as we shall see, but in

The Royal Abbey of Las Huelgas (Burgos), a major Cistercian convent founded in the 12th century

commenting on the advantage it was to have met so much opposition, she summed up the temper of Burgos very well. "Since this place is a kingdom, perhaps it wouldn't have noticed us had we entered silently." Mother Teresa's instinctive insight at its keenest!

Just as it was the Lord who began something in Galilee many centuries ago, so it was here: it was the encouragement he gave that enabled Teresa not to give in. "Be sure to make both of these foundations," he told her, referring to Palencia and Burgos.

And yet it appeared initially as if this would be an easy task. Take the archbishop to whom they looked for permission. Archbishop Cristóbal Vela was not only a native of Ávila and well acquainted with Teresa's work but also a relative and near neighbor who knew the family well.

He had formerly been a professor at Salamanca, then (from 1575) bishop in the Canary Islands, and had become archbishop of Burgos in 1580. The famous seminary he founded there was proof of his apostolic zeal.

It was precisely on the occasion of his installation as archbishop, when he was receiving the pallium from Bishop Álvaro de Mendoza, that the latter brought up the subject of a Carmelite house in Burgos. Not only did Archbishop Vela agree; he was positively delighted. As Teresa writes, "He had wanted one of these monasteries, because he knew how well the Lord was served in them" (F 31.3). No sign of a threat from this quarter then.

Another favorable factor in the undertaking was Teresa's close friendship with a rich and noble woman of that city, Doña Catalina de Tolosa. This devout widow had two sons and six daughters, and such was her love for Carmel that all of her children, except one daughter who died young, entered the Discalced Carmelites.

The Fountain of Flora (Fuente de la Flora); St. Teresa lived near here in the home of Doña Catalina de Tolosa when she arrived in Burgos.

St. Teresa's cell in the Carmel of Burgos

Here Teresa could count not only on Doña Catalina, her fortune, and her family but on her friends as well. There was Father Ripalda of the Society of Jesus, Doña María Manrique and her daughter, a son of hers who held a prominent position on the city council, and several other good and faithful servants of the Lord whom we will mention soon.

So, with the required backing of the Order and favorable prospects, the wheels of this new venture were set in motion. They had hardly started turning, though, when the project ran into two apparently formidable obstacles. First, the permission of the city council. Teresa and her little group had not sought the council's permission. But now the archbishop insisted on it, lest they encounter the kind of trouble they had had in Ávila. The second was the fact that the Carmelites had no endowment to guarantee an income.

It is worth recalling that the objections sometimes raised by cities to monasteries that relied on alms were prompted not by any dislike of the nuns themselves but by the fear that they would cause fewer donations to be given to other communities and all the groups would suffer as a result. Opposition from bishops was on the same grounds. Bishops preferred to refuse permission rather than see the nuns later half-starved or reduced to begging in the streets.

These two difficulties were taken care of by the good women mentioned above. Doña Catalina and Doña María prevailed upon María's councilmember son to bring up the matter of the needed permission with the city council. The following entry for November 4, 1581, is in the council's record book: "Having heard what Don Alonso has proposed, they said that permission will be granted as requested, since this work is so pious and necessary for this city."

Three days later Doña Catalina signed a document in which she guaranteed the support of the new community. "[The nuns] shall have," it read, "sufficient for their support, because I, for the service of Our Lord and the good of this city, will give them a house to live in, and I will see to their maintenance whenever necessary." Such generosity must have left Teresa speechless.

People were now advising Teresa to move quickly; there was talk of others wanting to found in Burgos too. Teresa was doubtful if her health could stand the rigors of a Burgos winter, so she decided to send the prioress of Palencia in her place. But the Lord thought otherwise: "One day . . . when raising this whole matter before the Lord . . . , He said: 'Pay no attention to the cold; I am the true warmth. The devil is marshaling all his forces against this foundation; you marshal Mine in its favor, and make sure you go personally for it will prove very beneficial'" (F 31.11).

The only person who didn't think everything was now perfectly straightforward was Father Gracián. He was provincial superior, and he insisted that Mother Teresa obtain the archbishop's permission in writing. She wrote again to her friends in Burgos, and they assured her that the matter had been sufficiently discussed with that prelate. Gracián relented, but only on

Entrance to the Hospital of the (Immaculate) Conception

condition that he would go with them in case any unforeseen difficulty should arise. How right he was!

They left Ávila on January 2; Teresa took along her niece Teresita and two nuns from Alba, one of them Tomasina Bautista, the new prioress. The first part of the trip was in driving sleet and snow. Teresa arrived in Medina "very tired and ill, with a large sore in her throat. She could eat only a little boiled mutton." Yet her own illness and fever were no obstacle to her healing others; her very presence cured the prioress of a fever that had kept her confined to bed and healed Sister Ana's cancer of the nose.

Then it was on to Valladolid. Teresa could barely speak, but she strongly approved of her nuns taking charge of a school for girls that a generous gentleman was anxious to endow. "Nothing serves the Lord better," she said, "than colleges where girls can be educated in recollection, virtue, and prayer. When they are brought up that way, God calls many of them to be nuns, and those who marry . . . make their husbands, children, and the whole family good" (*Peregrinación*, Dialogue 13). Unfortunately, this initiative never got off the ground; the Benedictine abbot of Valladolid insisted on its being under his jurisdiction.

Valladolid is a damp place, and Teresa moved on quickly to Palencia, where she received a rapturous welcome. When, after a six-day stay, she wanted to move on, everyone around her protested that the roads were impassable. That inner Voice, however, whispered, "It is all right to go; I will be with you."

Trusting in this word but keeping it to herself, Teresa moved on. It was fifty-nine miles to Burgos, and everyone thought them extremely rash for attempting the trip. They were now eight nuns, three friars, the bursar of the Palencia cathedral—and some *very* inexperienced mule drivers. Describing the dangers and misadventures of just this one trip in detail would take forever. But just a few examples give an idea: Sometimes the wagons got stuck in the deep, sticky mud. There was the time the nuns thought Father Gracián had fallen off his horse in the river; another when he thought Mother Teresa's wagon was being swept away by the current. And more than once the muleteers had to hold onto a wagon wheel for dear life to prevent a wagon from overturning. Nevertheless, they made it from one village to another, from one inn to another. In one of the latter, we are told, there wasn't even room to put Mother Teresa to bed.

And the worst was still to come. When they reached the pontoon bridge over the Arlanzón near Buniel, the river had become a veritable sea on all sides. Here their collective fears and anxiety reached their peak. The pontoons were narrow and almost covered with water, so they hired a guide to see them across. All a wagon had to do here was veer a little to the right or to the left and it would have been swept away. This is how Anne of St. Bartholomew, Mother Teresa's nurse, described the crossing: "Before entering this danger we went to confession, asked our Mother to bless us, and recited the Creed, just like people who were about to die. Seeing how discouraged we were, the saint laughed at us and said: 'Come on, daughters, what more could you ask for than to be martyrs here for the love of Our Lord?' Then she said that she would go first. If she drowned we were to turn back. In the end it pleased God to deliver us from this danger" (*Relación* 13).

This must have happened around noon on January 25. By mid-afternoon they had reached Burgos, but they made a detour to visit the famous Cristo de Burgos, a revered crucifix in a side chapel of the Burgos cathedral. They may have thought it better not to enter in the full light of day and were therefore just killing time. But it is not unreasonable to suppose

Inner cloister of the former 12th-century Royal Monastery of St. Augustine

that Teresa would have liked to pay a last visit to that impressive image of the crucified Christ that must have aroused all her memories and great love of the sacred humanity. After all, one day long ago she had had her Damascus experience. A real and personal encounter with Christ had changed her whole life.

Teresa's Christ was no dimly perceived refraction of a mystery; he was real. He was the Christ of the biblical scenes that so fascinated her. He was the Christ of the Eucharist where she saw him as clearly as his contemporaries had, whom she adored hidden there, and with whom she could "do business," especially just after Communion. He was at once her Master and Friend. He was the Christ who was involved and identified with that church so burdened with problems and evils, conflicts and defeats. He was the Christ of her inner life.

More than likely, we can be sure Teresa didn't spend her time wondering where this crucifix came from, or admiring its impressive realism. Impressed she no doubt was, but she would have gone beyond the image to God's infinite love reflected in it. She had allowed herself to become involved in this great drama herself, allowed God to go on loving humanity through her.

But to return to our story . . . One would have thought that with this infernal journey behind them, the devil's opposition would be at an end. Teresa describes the turn of events during the group's first twenty-four hours in Burgos:

It had been decided to proceed with the foundation immediately, and I had brought several letters from Canon Salinas (in Palencia) to his relatives and friends urging them to help us.

And so they did. They came the next day . . . to inquire how they could be of service. Since our only anxiety had been about the city council, we thought everything ought to go smoothly now. Since no one yet knew of our arrival (because the rain had been so heavy when we reached Doña Catalina's house) we thought it would be well to inform the archbishop of our arrival, so that we could then say the first Mass, as is my custom nearly everywhere. The weather prevented this.

"The Saint's Well" in the Carmel of Burgos

That night we rested in welcome comfort, thanks to this holy woman. Actually it did not do me any good; the large fire she had lit to dry our clothes . . . affected me so much that next day I could not even raise my head. I spoke from my bed to those who came. We hung a veil over an internal barred window for the purpose [of providing enclosure for Teresa]. Since this was a day on which it was essential to attend to business, this was very trying.

In the morning the father provincial went to ask the archbishop's blessing; we thought there would be no more to it than that. But he found him so angry at my coming without his permission that one would never have thought he had requested this himself . . . So he spoke of me in very angry terms to our father provincial. When [the archbishop] was forced to admit that it was he who had told me to come, he said that was only to discuss the matter with me alone, and not with so many nuns.

He dismissed the father provincial, telling him that if we didn't have revenues and a house of our own he would not grant his permission and that we could go back to where we had come from. (F 31.18–21)

A painting of the suffering Christ, from the saint's cell in Burgos

An antique
wooden clacker
in the Burgos
Carmel, used as
an alternative to
ringing a bell

Teresa's comment on all of this was, "and with the roads in such a fine state, and the weather so suitable!" We've seen the condition the roads were in; the archbishop's disposition was apparently no better.

What bothered Teresa was not so much the conditions he laid down as the protracted negotiations and the delay all this would involve. For the present, Doña Catalina's house became their convent. Since it had one rather fine room, which the Jesuits had used as a chapel when they first came to Burgos, Teresa and the nuns asked the archbishop if they could have Mass there. He would not allow Mass in a private house, he said. This meant that the nuns, who were supposedly cloistered, had to go out to a parish church for Mass on Sundays and holy days in the difficult Burgos winter.

Meanwhile, Teresa's friends were not idle. Canon Pedro Manso kept up the pressure on the archbishop, but the only answer he got was an impatient expression of surprise at the nuns being still in Burgos. Doña Catalina decided that a positive step would be to transfer ownership of her house to Mother Teresa and let her turn it into a monastery. The archbishop's officials dithered about it for a month and then pronounced the house unsuitable because of the dampness and its proximity to a noisy street. The same people refused to accept that Doña Catalina could maintain the community; they laid down 40,000 ducats as a minimum guarantee.

No wonder the Lord had insisted on Teresa coming in person! The devil appeared to be having a field day. The Lord's word in the midst of these disappointments was, "Now, Teresa, stand fast."

By now Lent was approaching and Father Gracián had preaching commitments in Valladolid. He couldn't bear to see the nuns tramping through the muddy streets to Mass, so before he left he looked for some way of remedying this situation. With the help of some interested parties in the civil administration, he succeeded in obtaining an attic for the nuns in the Hospital of the Immaculate Conception.

So, on February 23, almost a month after their arrival, Teresa and the little community moved their belongings to this new abode. It was poor, but at least they could now attend Mass from a balcony overlooking the hospital chapel and create their own convent atmosphere in the attic. But Teresa never forgot the generosity of the woman who fed them all for a month "as if they were all her children."

Teresa had more time now for house hunting and collecting money. She also paid frequent visits to the hospital patients and other religious communities in the city. Her simplicity and cheerfulness captivated people wherever she went. In fact, two nuns from another convent insisted on joining her Carmelite community.

Negotiations continued. Before he left Burgos, Father Gracián enlisted the help of an old friend in the medical profession, Don Antonio Aguiar, in the task of finding Mother Teresa a house. A difficult task, as available properties in the then-bustling city were at a premium. After several disappointments he struck gold: the Mansino property was being put up for sale. Mother Teresa was brought to look at it, and both agreed that it was ideal. What would they be asking? she wondered. Once again that unmistakable Voice took her to task: "Are you letting money hold you up?" They learned the price was very reasonable, and quickly closed on the purchase.

The deed was signed on March 12. By March 18, the community had taken residence in the new building. The total cost, for "two houses, yards,

The high altar in the church of the Carmel of Burgos

gardens, and fruit trees," was 1,290 ducats, payable over twelve months. The nuns had gotten a real bargain, and many in Burgos were soon wondering how they hadn't heard about it being up for sale. The owners were criticized for having let it go so cheaply, but they were quite happy to see their property become a monastery. St. Teresa was delighted, and even the archbishop claimed some credit—he had forced them to look for a house! He was pleased enough to visit the community but not, it would seem, to part with the long-sought permission to celebrate Mass in it. So for a little longer the nuns still had to go out to attend Mass.

On April 18, the archbishop finally gave in. Teresa relates, "He granted Dr. Manso permission to say Mass there the following day and reserve the Blessed Sacrament." The prior of the Dominican community "said the high Mass, to the accompaniment of many musicians, who," Teresa notes wryly, "came uninvited" (F 31.45).

Teresa brings this long account to an end as if she had been telling a fairy tale. Her joy that another oasis had been founded knows no bounds. Here is how she concludes the story of her last foundation:

> All our friends were very happy. In fact, so was most of the city, for many had been moved to pity by our plight. . . . The joy of Doña Catalina de Tolosa and all the sisters was such that I was moved to devotion, and I said to God: "Lord, as You see, all these servants of Yours want is to serve You and see themselves enclosed for Your sake in a place they will never leave." . . . Some days after the monastery had been founded the father provincial and I agreed that there were certain drawbacks to the endowment Doña Catalina had given this house. We put our trust in God and returned the money to her, without letting the archbishop know. . . .
>
> I did not want to leave until I saw whether there were persons desirous of entering this monastery. One day, after Communion, I was wondering about this, and the Lord said: "What are you wondering about? The work here is finished and you can safely go." From this I understood that they would lack nothing. . . . I got ready to leave, because I felt I was only

St. Mary's Arch, main gate of the city of Burgos

enjoying myself in this house. I might have more trouble elsewhere, but I would also do more good. (F 31.45–49)

Teresa did leave, but she had left her mark on Burgos. There are still some reminders of her physical presence there: a wall in the garden in which one can still see the *window of her cell*, the *cell* itself, the *well*, and a *portion of the church*. Among the relics are a *letter of hers*, a *veil*, one of her hemp-and-canvas *alpargatas,* a *jewelry box* that Doña Catalina gave her, and *some paintings*.

The Flemish artist Hye Hoys sketches the last of his series of drawings in the cell where St. Teresa died in Alba de Tormes

Alba de Tormes

JOURNEY'S END

Mother Teresa must have been feeling really tired. She had probably decided that Madrid, her cherished dream, would be the last foundation she would personally make. Now, duty called her to Ávila, where she was still prioress, for the profession of her niece Teresita, who was with her in Burgos.

Her presence in Burgos was not exactly superfluous but neither was it necessary. So, on about July 26, 1582, the feast of her beloved St. Anne, she set out with her niece and her nurse for Ávila.

First a stop at Palencia, where her health gave no cause for alarm. She stayed on there until mid-September. Then she moved on to Medina del Campo. Here an order from Father Antonio de Jesús, acting provincial in Father Gracián's absence, awaited her. She was to make a detour through Alba de Tormes because the Duchess of Alba wanted to see her again and have her pray for the safe delivery of her daughter-in-law. Everyone who was present on that occasion agreed that this was one of the most difficult acts of obedience Teresa had ever had to make, for by now she was really ill again.

The journey from Medina to Alba was in the usual covered wagon, a serious risk to her life. Sister Anne of St. Bartholomew, Teresa's secretary and nurse, found the trip a real torment, for she couldn't find any nourishing food. "When I saw that money could not buy what we needed, I couldn't look at our Mother without crying. She was like a corpse. . . . And all we had to give her were some figs. . . . While I was sobbing at seeing her in such great need . . . she comforted me saying the figs were delicious, that there were many poor people who couldn't enjoy such nice things" (*Autobiografía,* ms. 19389).

On September 29, they finally reached Alba. The sisters knew how ill Teresa was and were waiting anxiously. They would have loved to talk with her, but they had the good sense to put her to bed immediately. "God help me," she said, "how tired I feel! In twenty years I've never had to go to bed as early as this." Teresa took to her bed, never to rise again. She knew death was near and prepared herself to welcome it.

October 3 came. The sisters were praying and weeping by her bedside. Father Antonio administered the last rites. The duchess was there, serving what little food Teresa could eat, giving her medicine, adjusting her pillows and bed covers. But there was no containing this illness. Between bouts of unconsciousness, loss of speech, and violent fluctuations in her pulse rate, Teresa spoke her last words, her voice full of emotion but getting weaker by the minute. According to her faithful nurse, Blessed Anne,

[Mother Teresa] asked for the Blessed Sacrament. . . . When they were taking it away she sat up in the bed with a great surge of spirit and said joyfully: "My Lord, it is time to be going. Very well, Your will be done."

She thanked God unceasingly that she was a daughter of the church and was dying in it. She said she hoped for salvation through the merits of Christ, and asked us all to pray God to forgive her sins and to regard His own mercy rather than them. . . .

On the evening of the day she died Father Antonio told me to go and get myself something to eat. I had no sooner left than the Holy Mother became very restless and began looking all about her. The Father asked if she wanted me to come back and she nodded. They called me, and when she saw me she smiled at me. She affectionately took my hands and laid her head between my arms. I held her there until she died. (*Autobiografía*)

It was October 4, 1582. Teresa was sixty-seven years old.

Today her body lies in the monastery chapel at Alba, and through a little window to one side of the altar one can view the room in which she died.

In 1584, when Father Gracián was making a visitation, Teresa's tomb was opened. According to her biographer, Francisco de Ribera, despite the large quantity of quicklime that had been poured on top of the coffin, "the body was as fresh and intact as if it had only just been buried."

Teresa's travels were still not over even after her death. In 1585, the general chapter of the Discalced Carmelites decreed that the foundress's body be transferred to St. Joseph's, Ávila. On November 25 of that year, the coffin was solemnly transported to Ávila. However, the Duke of Alba petitioned Pope Sixtus IV to have the body returned to Alba. So, the following August, back it went again.

So great was the fame of Teresa's holiness that the juridical procedures for beatification began soon after her death. She was beatified on April 24, 1614, and canonized on March 12, 1622, by Pope Gregory XV. Teresa of Jesus was the only woman among the illustrious group of saints canonized that day: St. Isidore the farmer, St. Ignatius of Loyola, St. Francis Xavier, and St. Philip Neri.

The cell where St. Teresa died in the Carmel of Alba; it is now an oratory

Her remains, in the Church of the Annunciation adjacent to the monastery, are located above the main altar in a rich marble and gold sarcophagus, a gift of King Ferdinand IV and his queen, Doña Bárbara de Braganza.

St. Teresa's Writings

The saint's writings are about her life and her teaching on the spiritual and religious life. None of her books was written on her own initiative; she wrote only on the orders of her superiors and confessors. In fact, she often complained about being required to write, protesting that she could be more useful to the community with her spinning.

Teresa's works have gone into thousands of editions in a wide variety of languages. The first Spanish edition was edited by Fray Luis de León in 1588. Here is how he introduced it: "I doubt if anything has been written in our language to equal these writings for purity and ease of style, for happy choice of words, and an unaffected elegance which is so entirely pleasing. Whenever I read them I am filled anew with admiration. To mention only two of the many benefits to be derived from reading them, they make the path of virtue attractive, and set the reader on fire with love of [Teresa] and love of God."

Her principal writings are as follows:

THE BOOK OF HER LIFE

Teresa was almost fifty when she began writing this book, sometimes called her autobiography. She herself often referred to it as a "book of the mercies of the Lord." Teresa does give some autobiographical information but treats mainly of the interior life, offering a detailed presentation on prayer, its nature, stages, and effects. It includes her description of the founding of her first monastery, St. Joseph's (San José) in Ávila. It was written by order of her confessors between 1562 and 1565. The original is preserved in El Escorial, the famous monastic library near Madrid.

THE WAY OF PERFECTION

Written during the first years that Teresa guided the fledgling community of St. Joseph's, Ávila (1562–1567), this is a practical book of advice to help initiate her nuns into the life of prayer. Here Teresa is a master teacher, describing prayer as the purpose and goal of Discalced Carmelite life. It was designed as a manual to accompany and explain her Primitive Constitutions, written during the same period. It includes a commentary on the Our Father. The first version is preserved in El Escorial; the second is in the Valladolid Carmel.

THE INTERIOR CASTLE

Considered Teresa's masterpiece, she wrote this last work in just a few months in 1577, five years before her death. At this point in her life, she had been granted the highest mystical graces; this is the fruit of her experience. Teresa describes her own inner journey using the image of a castle. The soul journeys progressively through seven mansions, or dwelling places, until finally reaching the center, where, now transformed, it is united with God. The original manuscript is in the Seville Carmel.

THE BOOK OF THE FOUNDATIONS

Teresa wrote the *Foundations* as an historical record as the various monasteries were being founded between 1562 and 1582. Its documentary importance is indisputable, but its pages are also a treasure house of spiritual and psychological insight. This is the foundress as entertaining travel writer, sometimes wandering off topic and inaccurate but always a great narrator. With a flair for detail and characteristic humor, she describes the opposition and hardships she and the nuns and friars went through in establishing these monasteries, as well as the kindness of those who helped them. In her famous digressions, she gives advice to the nuns. As she narrates the various events, the reader is impressed by the divine atmosphere that pervades the narrative and by the great humanity, humor, and total practicality of this woman who lived in such close intimacy with God. The original manuscript is in El Escorial.

MEDITATIONS ON THE SONG OF SONGS

Writing about erotic love poetry, even if it's in the Bible, was incredibly daring for a 16th-century woman, especially a nun! At a time when commentaries on Scripture were either censored by the Inquisition or forbidden outright, Teresa wrote this brief but powerful treatise to share some of the consolation and understanding she experienced when reading verses of this book, which were included in the Little Office of the Blessed Virgin that the nuns prayed. On orders from a nervous confessor, Teresa burned the original manuscript. Happily for us, her savvy nuns had already made copies. It was published in 1611.

LETTERS

Many say the best way to get to know Teresa is through her letters. Here she's at her most human: consoling (and scolding), humorously describing people and situations, pleading her cause with kings and cardinals, and dealing with difficult people and business matters from Spain to Latin America. It has been estimated that in the last twenty years of her life, Teresa must have written between 15–20,000 letters. Through the almost 500 that have come down to us, we meet Teresa's fascinating galaxy of friends and colleagues, nuns and friars, religious leaders, family members, and opponents. Whether written to family, her nuns, or the king, her letters are all charmingly simple and spontaneous. Their clarity and sincerity give us insight into Teresa's personality, intellect, and great heart and soul.

SPIRITUAL TESTIMONIES

This is a collection of sixty-five written reports (known in Spanish as the *Relaciónes*) left by Teresa about her spiritual experiences. There are six longer accounts of her state of soul, as well as numerous shorter reports and fragments in which she usually describes some particular grace or counsel given her by the Lord. She tells us that some of these were written down at the Lord's command. Teresa composed three of the longer accounts (1–3) for her confessors before she completed her *Life*; the other three are from a later date. The final long account was destined for a former confessor and written in 1581. There are some excellent descriptions of mystical prayer and, in testimony 59, an interesting summary of its stages. The originals of the various documents are scattered rather widely; the largest collection of them is at St. Joseph's, Ávila.

SOLILOQUIES

Also known in Spanish as the *Exclamaciónes*, these seventeen outpourings of fervent love for God were first published in Luis de León's edition of the saint's works, issued in Salamanca in 1588. He titled them, "Meditations or exclamations of the soul to God written by Mother Teresa of Jesus in the year 1569 on different days according to the spirit Our Lord gave her after Communion." Because of the similarity of these to the literary genre they express, the critical English edition (Kavanaugh-Rodriguez) uses the simple title *Soliloquies* in place of the more elaborate *Exclamations of the Soul to God*.

POEMS

These thirty-one poems, some intended to be sung, were never meant for publication. Teresa wrote them either to entertain her nuns or to celebrate some event, usually a feast day. She made no claims to poetic talent. A few, however, have acquired some standing, especially "Aspirations toward Eternal Life" (I die because I do not die) and "In the Hands of God," with its powerful refrain, "I am Yours and born for You, What do You want of me?" The latter was used by the Carmelite Order as the theme for the fifth centenary of St. Teresa's birth, celebrated in 2015.

GUIDELINES FOR THE VISITATION OF CONVENTS

This short work seeks to advise both nuns and their visiting superiors on how to make the visitation of a Discalced Carmelite community spiritually profitable. Father Jerome Gracián asked her to write this, feeling that her experience would be an invaluable guide to others. She wrote it in Toledo in 1576. The original is in El Escorial.

Doctor of the Universal Church

As if to put a further stamp of approval on all that has been noted above, on St. Teresa's feast day, October 15, 1967, Pope Paul VI announced his intention of declaring St. Teresa a "Doctor of the Universal Church."

This unexpected announcement was a complete surprise because until then no woman had ever been accorded this official church distinction. In fact, the first person to be surprised at what flowed from Teresa's pen was herself. "I see clearly," she confessed, "that it is not I who am saying this; I don't arrange it in my mind and afterward I don't know how I succeeded in saying it" (L 14.8). And elsewhere: "Many of the things I write here do not come out of my head; my heavenly Master has been saying them" (L 39.8).

The appointed day arrived. On September 27, 1970, in the presence of official delegations from all over the world and thousands of the faithful, Pope Paul VI made this solemn pronouncement:

THEREFORE, IN COMPLETE CERTAINTY AND AFTER MATURE DELIBERATION, WITH THE FULLNESS OF THE APOSTOLIC AUTHORITY, WE PROCLAIM SAINT TERESA OF JESUS, VIRGIN FROM ÁVILA, DOCTOR OF THE UNIVERSAL CHURCH.

With the placing of this supreme seal of the church on her "message," Teresa's travels were truly now complete.

St.Teresa's Foundations (1562–1582)

About Us

ICS Publications, based in Washington, D.C., is the publishing house of the Institute of Carmelite Studies (ICS) and a ministry of the Discalced Carmelite Friars of the Washington Province (U.S.A.) The Institute of Carmelite Studies promotes research and publication in the field of Carmelite spirituality, especially about Carmelite saints and related topics. Its members are friars of the Washington Province.

Discalced Carmelites are a worldwide Roman Catholic religious order comprised of friars, nuns, and laity—men and women who are heirs to the teaching and way of life of Teresa of Avila and John of the Cross, dedicated to contemplation and to ministry in the church and the world.

Information about their way of life is available through local diocesan vocation offices, or from the Discalced Carmelite Friars vocation directors at the following addresses:

Washington Province:
1525 Carmel Road, Hubertus, WI 53033

California-Arizona Province:
P.O. Box 3420, San Jose, CA 95156

Oklahoma Province:
5151 Marylake Drive, Little Rock, AR 72206

Visit our websites at:

www.icspublications.org   and   *www.ocdfriarsvocation.org*